D1789462

Shell Designs

CHRISTINE HARAGAN was born in Farnborough Kent in 1952. Christine Haragan was educated at Homewood Secondary School — from where she went on to study Hairdressing — owning and working in her own salon until 1978.

Having had no formal education in art it was her passionate hobby and interest from an early age. Art is now her full time occupation — her interest in sea shells has developed since 1970 due to her desire to see these natural objects of beauty glorified.

Shell Designs

Christine Haragan

To Dad

In the same Midas Craft Library

Coal Hole Rubbings
The Story of an Artefact in our Streets by Lily Goddard
Pressed Flower Craft by Joyce Fenton
Shell Designs by Christine Haragan
Photo Montage by Lee Campion
Gems, Minerals and Rocks — Creative Uses by Alan Major

Edited by Georgina Hulme

All rights reserved. No part of this publication may be reproduced, stored in a retrieval system, or transmitted in any form or by any means, electronic, mechanical, photocopying, recording or otherwise, without the prior permission of Midas Books.

First published in 1980 by
Midas Books
12 Dene Way, Speldhurst,
Tunbridge Wells, Kent TN3 0NX

©Christine Haragan 1980

ISBN 0 85936 137 3

Designed by Paul Turner

Filmset in Souvenir by Tunbridge Wells Typesetting Services
Printed in Great Britain by offset lithography by G. A. Pindar & Son Ltd., Scarborough
Bound by Western Book Co. Ltd., Maesteg, Glamorgan

CONTENTS

INTRODUCTION

We have all at some time walked along a beach and picked up shells and it is probably their colour that first attracts us. Shells have fascinated and intrigued man since he first walked on earth and he has used molluscs and shells in numerous ways, as food, tools and as objects of art. Molluscs inhabit all the waters, beaches and mud flats of our earth and we know of over a million species, 600 of which are found around the coast of the British Isles.

The molluscs first practical use to man was food. Large quantities of clam shells have been found in the middens of sites occupied by Neolithic Man. Arrow heads and scrapers were also made from shell in the parts of the world where there was no suitable flint or stone. Some larger shells such as the large clam and the cut helmet shells were used as cooking utensils.

The little 'money' cowrie shell served as currency for centuries. It is thought that China used them as early as 2,000 BC until 600 BC when they were replaced by metal coins. The little 'money' cowries were ideal for this particular use, because of their uniform shape and natural abundance.

Central African tribes used these shells as money up until the late 1800s. Their value was set on the principle that 1 cow = 2,500 cowries, 1 chicken = 25 cowries, and 1 tobacco pipe = 20 cowries. The Africans showed their wealth by making the cowries into elaborate belts and head-dresses which were worn at important social gatherings.

The cowrie was dropped from use because of the large amounts that had to be exchanged making it difficult to carry and store them. A perfect example of this was a man from Dacca who, in 1756, when the cowrie was worth 1 rupee, wanted a bungalow built and had to pay several million cowries — very inconvenient.

Women have adorned themselves with jewellery ever since 900 BC. Sea shells played a very important part in this as their natural colours and shapes made them ideal. Through the centuries they have been used as inlays in wood and ivory and their shapes have been imitated in paintings and pottery and even in the magnificent mosaic floors of the Greeks. The Victorian era saw all kinds of objects decorated and covered with shells, from little pill boxes to grand pianos.

Man has always coveted the natural beauty and colour of shells, along with bird feathers and minerals and, in some cases, very high value and importance has been placed upon them. Cameo and black pearls, gold and silver, diamonds and ostrich feathers are some of the worlds most precious and beautiful materials, all of which have been made by Nature.

Chapter 1

SEA SHELLS

Sea shells are found in every ocean and sea of the world and they vary greatly in all aspects — colour, size, shape and habitat. It is this marvellous variation that first attracts collectors to them, only to start them on a lifetime hobby.

There are numerous volumes available on the subject of sea shells for the collector, but this book is designed to give you some ideas and information on how to use shells. This brief chapter aims just to help you understand and increase your interest in the world of sea shells.

What is a shell?

A shell, generally speaking, is the protective home or coat of the invertebrate animals known as molluscs, but not all molluscs have shells. For instance, squids, octopuses and slugs have no shell at all, but they are still molluscs and they belong to the **Cephalopoda** class. The shells of molluscs are composed of the same chemical that is the basis of such rocks as chalk and limestone — crystals of calcium carbonate.

The mollusc increases the size of its shell by depositing the crystals in layers around the edge of its shell. It does this by using special glands, which are positioned around the edge of its soft fleshy mantle on the pallial line. See figure 1.

Classification of molluscs

All molluscs belong to one of the largest groups in the animal kingdom — **Phylum mollusca** containing over 100,000 species. This group is divided into six major classes.

Gastropoda — or univalves. This is the largest class of molluscs containing about 80,000 species. They all have a one-piece shell which is usually coiled, but a large number are cap shaped such as the limpet. Other examples of univalves are Murex, Whelks, Conches and Snails. See figure 2.

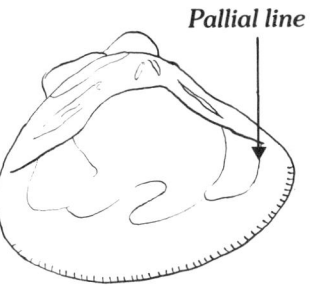

Pallial line

Figure 1.

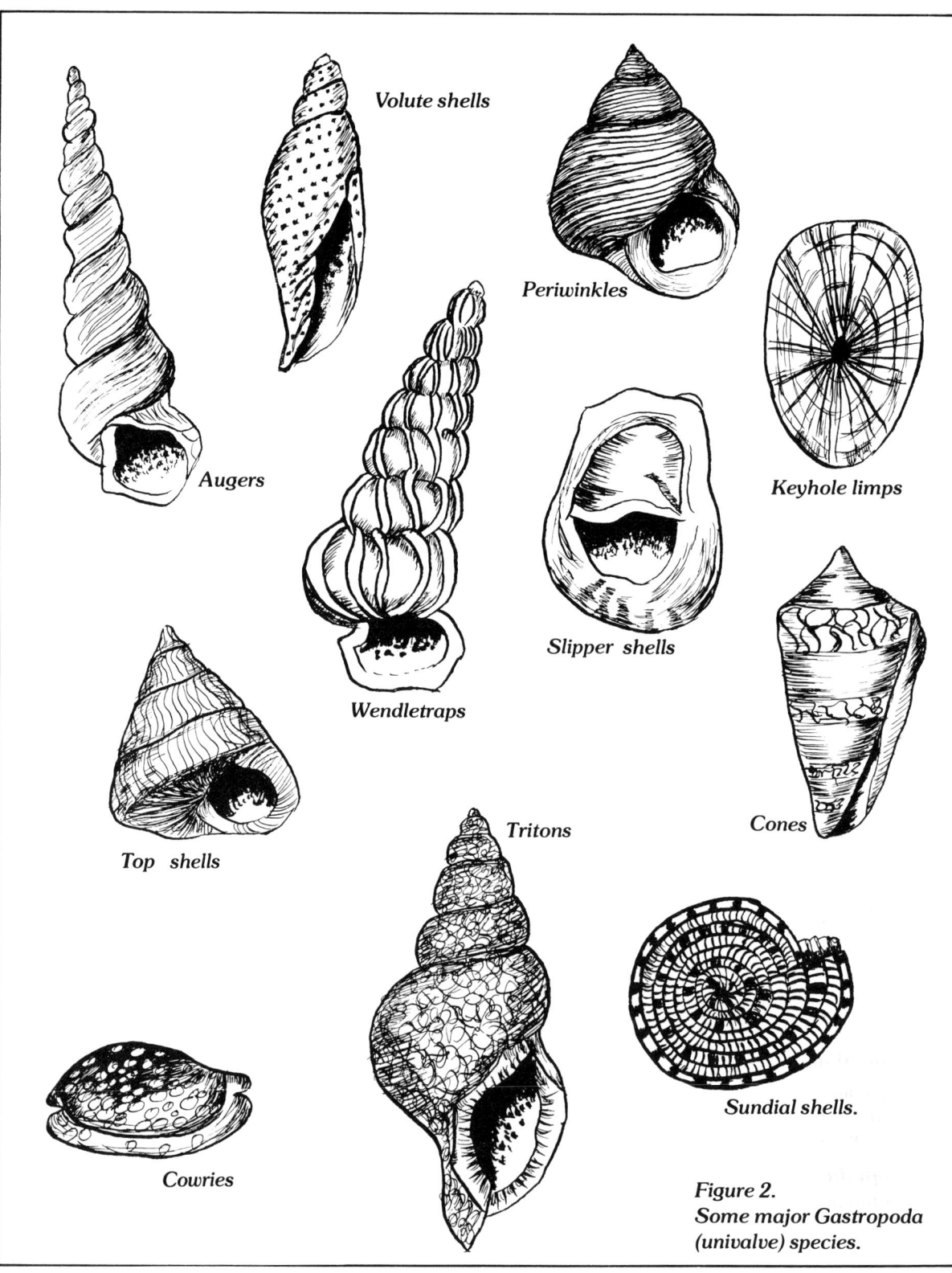

Volute shells

Periwinkles

Keyhole limps

Augers

Wendletraps

Slipper shells

Cones

Top shells

Tritons

Cowries

Sundial shells.

Figure 2.
Some major Gastropoda
(univalve) species.

Most of these univalves crawl around on a large flat foot and have tentacles with eyes placed at the base or on the tip. In their feeding habits they may be carnivorous, herbivorous or even scavengers. Univalves were the only molluscs to venture onto land about 30,000 years ago leaving us with snails and slugs.

Asymmetrical animal fossils have been found in large numbers dating back to the Lower Cambrian Period about 600 million years ago! This makes them the oldest class of mollusc known to man.

Bivalvia — bivalves include such familiar molluscs as Oysters, Cockles, Clams and Mussels. See figure 3. This is the second largest class containing approximately 20,000 species and they are, as the name suggests, animals with a two-piece shell, hinged on one edge. They move by means of a very muscular wedge-shaped foot which they also use to attach themselves to the surface of rocks. Bivalves are mainly herbivorous.

Despite the size of this class there is no evidence to suggest that bivalves have ever ventured onto land. Bivalve fossils have been found dating back to the Middle Cambrian Period about 550 million years ago.

Razor shells

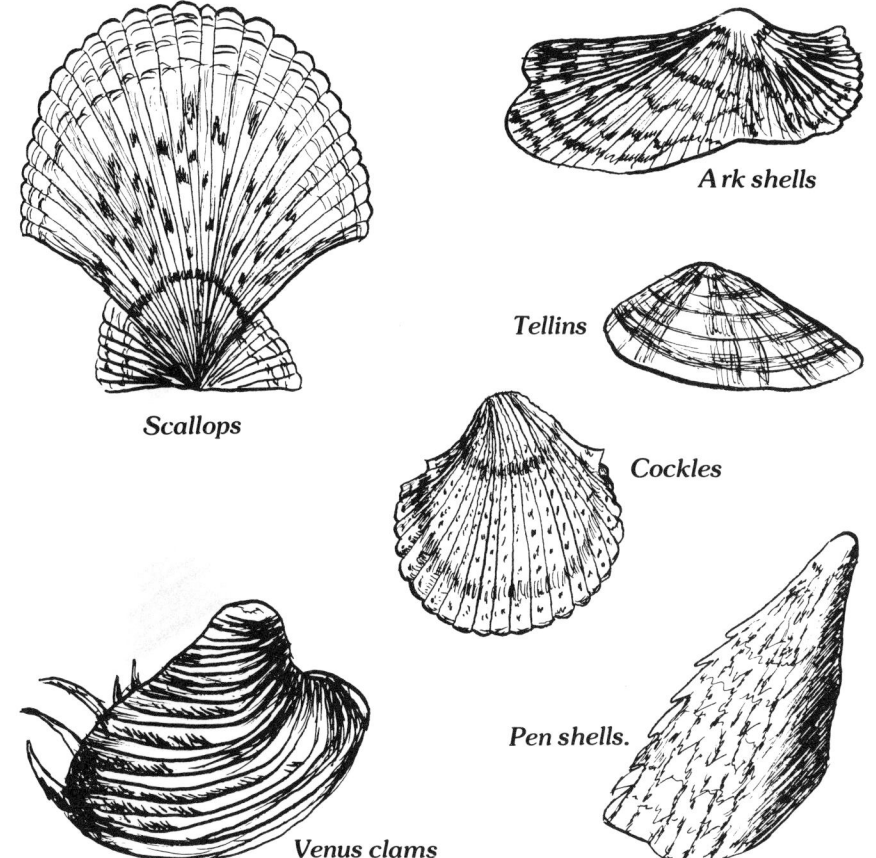

Ark shells

Tellins

Mussel shells

Scallops

Cockles

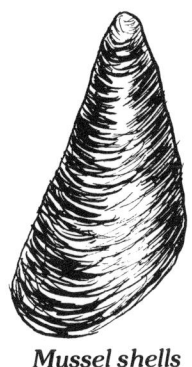

Pen shells.

Venus clams

Figure 3.
Some major Bivalve
species.

Figure 4.
Nautilus

Cephalopoda This is a smaller class containing around 400 species, most of which are without a shell at all, for example, Squids, Octopuses and Cuttlefish. The Nautilus and Spirula are an exception to the rule because they have a one-piece shell that is chambered. See figure 4.

Cephalopoda all have arms or tentacles, which may have rows of suckers upon them, these suckers help to propel them through water at speed. Cephalopoda are mainly carnivorous and have a long history stretching back about 400 million years; at which time the nautilus was abundant but its numbers have since diminished drastically to just three species.

Scaphopoda — or Tusk shells are one of the minor classes with only 500 species. They are recognisable immediately by their shape which resembles a small elephant's tusk. See figure 5.

The Tusk shell lies partially buried on the sandy seabed with its posterior end exposed, from which tentacle-like filaments extend, capturing food and passing it through to the mouth. They live in all depths of water ranging from a few feet to the great fathoms of the oceans.

Tusk shells vary greatly in size, some are hardly the length of a grain of rice and others can reach up to 13cm (5in).

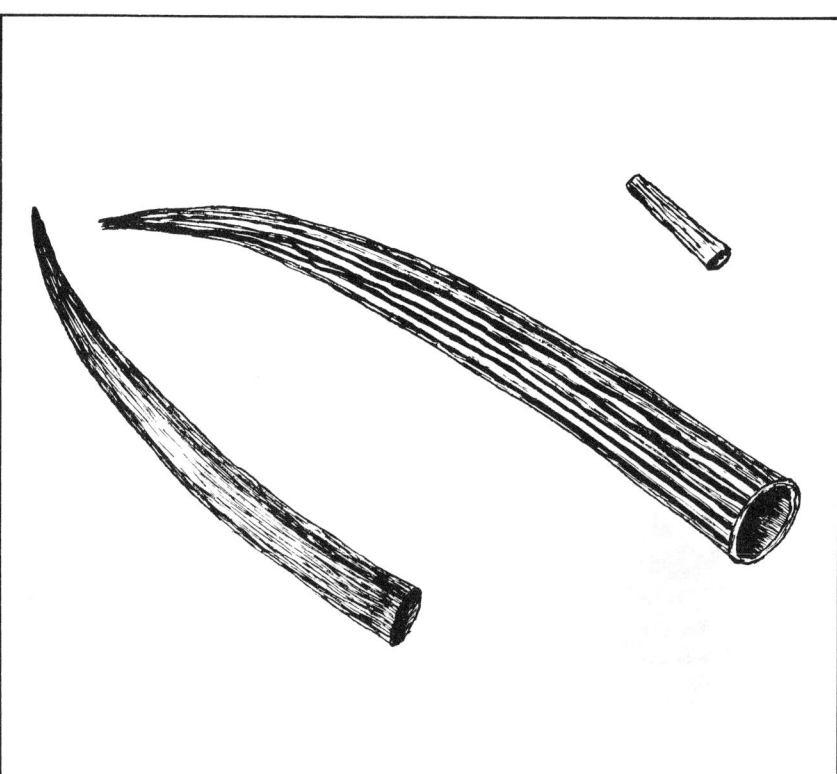

Figure 5.

Amphineura — or Chitons sometimes called 'coat of mail shell'. See figure 6.

Chitons are another minor class of about 500 species. They are unique because their shells are comprised of eight separate sections that overlap, so giving them the name 'coat of mail shells'.

They are herbivores and live on or under rocks and stones feeding on algae; if dislodged from their rock they will curl up like an armadillo for protection.

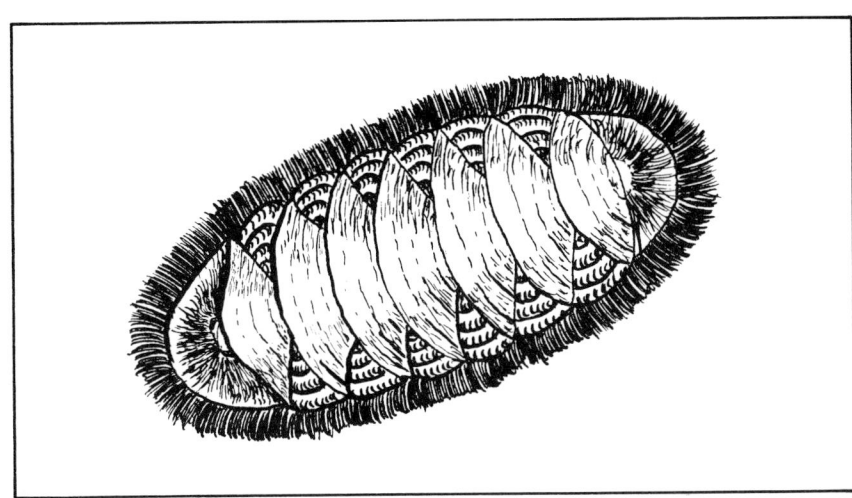

Figure 6.

Monoplacophora — or gastroverms are the smallest of all the classes containing only six species. See figure 7.

Gastroverms are the most primitive of all molluscs and they are impossible to collect as they live in very deep waters and have only been collected on rare occasions by research vessels. They were thought to have become extinct some 280 million years ago, until 1957 when one was dredged up off the coast of West Mexico.

They have simple Limpet-shaped shells, less than 2.5cm (1in) in size, and are very thin and fragile.

Collecting shells

Molluscs not only inhabit all the world's seas, but they have also invaded the fresh and brackish waters of the world and some live very successfully on land.

The marine molluscs which live on the beach or in the shallow waters are the easiest to collect, but care must always be exercised not to over-collect from one beach as this can easily alter the natural balance of that particular shore.

For this particular craft we really only need to collect empty shells which can be found in large quantities along the middle shore of most beaches. Collecting empty shells means that you can collect as many as

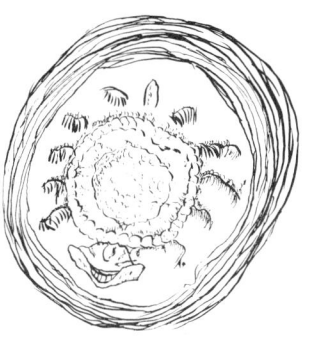

Figure 7.

you require and it will not upset the balance. However, it is still interesting to collect one or two live specimens, as they make good centre pieces for many designs.

As we are mainly concerned with collecting empty shells only a plastic bucket or a large, thick plastic bag is necessary. If, however, you are thinking of collecting live molluscs, you will also need tools for digging them out, so take with you the following items: A strong, plastic bag or bucket, a small spade or trowel for digging out bivalves, and you may also find that a kitchen knife is useful for prising gastropods off the rocks.

Whilst you are collecting shells and molluscs, keep an eye open for attractive pebbles, driftwood, cork, seaweed or pieces of glass worn smooth by the sea, as these can all be used in conjunction with shells in your designs. Never pass by the broken and sea worn shells as these are sometimes very beautiful and usable shapes. This applies especially to gastropods.

It is a good idea to persuade friends and aquaintances to bring you back any shells they may collect whilst on their holidays. Local fishermen too are usually very helpful and will often let you have any shells of molluscs they may catch.

Shell species that cannot be collected may be bought from specialist shell shops. They usually provide a price list from which you can buy by mail order. Some shops sell small bags of shells which are very useful for mass backgrounds or you can even buy bags of mixed shells.

Cleaning your shells

Now that the shells have been collected, it is probable that some of them will still contain live molluscs and they must be cleaned as soon as possible. The smell of decaying molluscs is very pungent and enough to put off even the keenest of shell collectors.

The cleaning of shells must be done with great care because their beauty and preservation largely depends on this stage being carried out correctly. There are six methods of cleaning: Freezing, boiling, preserving, salting, rotting out and bleaching.

Freezing, boiling and bleaching are the best methods. They are easy and can all be carried out at home or in a hotel if you are on holiday. The remaining three methods are mainly used by professionals when trying to save one or two perfect specimens for a show collection.

Freezing

Freezing is a relatively modern method of cleaning, and has only become widely used in the last twenty years. This method is popular because it is a convenient way of killing live molluscs, also there are very few houses or hotels that do not have freezing facilities. It is very quick for the mollusc concerned and does little to harm the beauty of the shell.

First, put the mollusc-filled shells into a plastic bag, tie it and place it in the lower part of the refrigerator for about five hours. Next, move them to the freezing compartment for two or three days.

Thaw the shells out by putting them back into the lower compartment for approximately five hours and follow this with a soak in cold water. This method is carried out gradually so as to avoid cracking the enamel-like gloss on the shell.

When they have been completely thawed out, the meat from any univalve will usually come out easily with the help of a safety pin. Always remember to lift the dead mollusc out from the shell by using an unwinding, corkscrew action. If you try to lift it straight out it will probably break off and the piece left behind will be extremely difficult to remove. Bivalves are easily cleaned by just scraping with a knife.

Boiling

This is also a very quick and easy method. It will be found that the molluscs do not scream as do crabs and lobsters because the mollusc-filled shells should always be put into cold water and brought to the boil gradually. This stops any cracking or crazing on the shiny surface of the shell. When they are ready, all shells should be brought down from the boil gradually and allowed to cool naturally.

Univalves are usually ready to be taken off the boil after ten minutes and when they have cooled down, extract the dead molluscs with a safety pin as previously described.

Bivalves only take between four and six minutes, but of course their size may alter these times. Once they have been allowed to cool down, scrape out the dead molluscs with a knife, making sure that every piece is cleaned away.

Bivalves will always gape after death, so if the shell is needed in the closed position, place an elastic band around it after cleaning and leave for a few hours.

Bleaching

Many of the shells picked up will be empty and these are easily and quickly cleaned by soaking in warm, soapy water. Any commercial washing-up liquid is satisfactory. After they have had a good soak, it may be necessary to give them a light scrub with a toothbrush to remove seaweed and sand, etc.

Some of the shells will have been stained by seaweed or tar and may even have a chalky deposit on the inside. The best method for removing this is to bleach the shells. Some consider that bleach is too harsh and damaging, but as the shells are intended for use, and not for a specimen collection, this method is quite satisfactory. Soak the shells overnight in full-strength bleach and then wash them well in warm, soapy water followed by two or three rinses until all trace of the bleach has gone.

If the shells have lost their shine, and this can happen for any number of reasons, then rub a little baby oil over the shell. However, if they are to be used in designs, do not put oil on any part of the shell which has to be glued as this may prevent the shell from adhering easily to the background.

Tides

When collecting shells and molluscs, it is wise to take into account the local tides. A little knowledge of tides can be very helpful because they can either assist or hinder your collecting expeditions. There is nothing more depressing than arriving at the beach ready to collect shells, only to find that it is high tide. It can also be dangerous if you are collecting under cliffs, as you can easily be cut off by the sea.

Tides and weather play a large part in the success of your shell collecting expeditions. Some of your excursions are likely to be more rewarding than others, such as at a very low tide when shells which are normally covered will be exposed. Another prime shell collecting time is after there have been gales and storms, or a particularly high tide such as a spring tide when it is quite likely that you will find molluscs which normally live off-shore. These varying conditions cause molluscs to be washed up, making it easy for you to collect.

Tide tables are helpful if you want to time your visits correctly for a low tide. The tides are influenced by both the sun and the moon as they exert a gravitational pull on the waters of the world, causing movement towards themselves. The tidal movements are complicated and vary from one part of the world to another. Some places, such as the Mediterranean Sea, have hardly any tides at all.

Although tide tables sound very complicated, you will find them quite easy to understand. The tables can be obtained from any stationers or may be printed in local newspapers. You will also usually find that the local coastguards office is very helpful.

It is best to arrive at the coast about 1½ hours before low tide, then it is possible to follow the tide as it goes out, enabling you to collect specimens which might otherwise get trodden underfoot.

Some tidal terms

High water occurs approximately 6 hours 13 minutes after *Low water.*

Spring tides occur a little after both new and full moons, about every two weeks. The height and range of these will be greater than usual.

Perigee is when the moon reaches its nearest point to earth and coincides with a full or new moon, resulting in an abnormally wide-ranging spring tide.

Neap tides are smaller than usual and occur halfway between each spring tide.

Chapter 2

USING SHELLS

Where to find sea shells

Distribution of marine molluscs is determined by basic living conditions. These include climate, ocean currents, temperature, depth of water and the molluscs' individual feeding habits. These factors prevent molluscs of different types spreading throughout the seas of the world. For example, a species that thrives in cold, sunless, turbulent seas, with a limited food supply, is unlikely to be found in warm, calm, sunlit waters. It will also be found that the shells of molluscs living in warm waters are usually more brightly coloured and marked than those of molluscs living in cold waters.

For those of you who would like to find out details of distribution in any particular area, the appropriate local authorities or museums are usually very helpful, and there are also a number of books and journals available on the subject. If you intend to take up shell collecting in order to make a specimen collection, then it is advisable to join a shell club or conchological society.

It is as well to know the types of shells you are likely to come across on a particular kind of shore, so here are some general guidelines to follow.

Sandy shores

Sandy shores yield the best harvest of empty shells. Almost all types will be found here, so this is the best kind of shore to use if you are collecting shells for art work.

All molluscs adapted for a burrowing existence find sandy shores and sea beds ideal. These are largely bivalves or Tusk shells, but a good many gastropods also like this type of shore.

Most of the molluscs live just below the surface or only half buried, which is very convenient. However, some others, such as Razor shells, dig themselves in very deep and a spade is necessary if you intend to collect live specimens.

You will find all types of Harp shell, Volutes, Olives, Tellins, Cockles and numerous others on these shores.

Rocky shores

Despite the often extreme conditions on rocky shores they are surprisingly rich in molluscs and shells. These molluscs have to be able to go without water for hours or even weeks, as they live attached to rocks and the tide may only reach them once a day, or even less.

Bivalves, such as mussels, will be found secured to rocks at the low water zone. Other bivalves will be found squeezing into the crevices between, or even burrowing into the rocks. Periwinkles are often found well above the high tide line. As Limpets, Nerites and Chitons are hunters, they move around at night finding food and then return to their original place ready for the next day.

Some small gastropods attach themselves to seaweed and if you turn damp seaweed over you can usually find a host of Periwinkles and Top shells.

Coral reefs

None of man's achievements can compare with the Great Barrier Reef off the east coast of Australia, which is 1,900 km (1,200 miles) long. It is built entirely from the skeletons of tiny creatures called polyps.

Coral provides a food-rich habitat for some of the world's most beautiful molluscs including Volutes, Mitres, Cowries, Cones, Conches and Date Mussels. Very few empty shells will be found here as they are usually broken after being thrashed about by the sea on the reef.

Tropical mangroves

Dense mangroves thrive on the silt and mud which accumulates in the estuaries and lagoons of the tropics. They are dark, quiet and cool, making them a haven for various forms of life, including molluscs.

The Zebra Cowrie can be found in the mangroves of the West Indies and the yellow Money Cowrie in the Pacific.

Deep waters

Many of the molluscs that live in the deep waters will never be washed up on shore, so they have to be collected by professional divers or even dredged. They include the Spindle Tibia and the Precious Wentletrap. These shells may be bought from any specialist shop.

Shingle shores

Shingle is the poorest area for finding molluscs, and even empty shells are usually damaged because they are being continually moved and pounded by the sea.

Identifying your shells

Once the shells have been washed and cleaned, let them dry on a towel or on blotting paper. The next step is to divide them into their respective families. A good idea is to have a clearly illustrated book on shell identification. However, it is not necessary to identify individual shells by name because they can easily be grouped together by their shapes. Only a little knowledge of their names is required, but working with shells becomes more pleasurable if you have this knowledge.

All shells are universally known by their Latin names. Their family name appears first and then their species, such as the English Whelk which is classified as: family — **Buccinum** and species — **Undatum.** This can often be followed by the name of the person who first discovered and named the shell. Most shells are given a common name which I shall use throughout my book wherever possible.

Storing your shells

When the shells have been identified, it is most convenient to put them into separate containers according to size and colour. The best way to do this, is to take an individual family and separate the shells into groups by size. Also, if they differ greatly in colour, such as the Baltic Tellin, then divide them further by colour — whites, yellows and pinks.

Dividing the shells thus, protects them as well as making it easier to find a particular shell at any given time. This saves you rummaging

Plate 1

Above: plate 2

Below: plate 3

through your shells, tossing them about, breaking or chipping them; it also prevents a lot of frustration.

Some families, especially the bivalves such as the Thin Tellin are very delicate so I lie these on cotton wool in their boxes.

Now the shells have been named, stored and divided into families, sizes and colours, and placed in separate containers, arrange them on the working surface, leaving a space immediately in front of you for your background board. It is a good idea to place the containers in a semi-circle so that all the shells are within easy reach at any one time and are clearly visible.

Tools and equipment

Working with sea shells needs very little specialised equipment. In fact almost all the tools necessary can be found in most homes or classrooms. After a little experience of working with shells you may even find that you are able to devise and improvise your own tools. It is a completely personal thing. I use my tweezers for nearly all work, whereas others prefer a cocktail stick. Whatever you use, it must be comfortable and almost an extension of your fingers.

For some shell work you may find that you will need to drill holes. A handyman's hand drill is particularly suitable for this as it is easier to regulate the speed. The best drill bits to use are the dual purpose high speed steel twist drills.

When making a symmetrical shell pattern you may need the help of a protractor, a pair of compasses, a rule and pencil to obtain a good line on which to set the shells.

Adhesives

There is a considerable difference of opinion as far as adhesives are concerned. It is really a matter of personal preference, and the best thing is to try several until you find the one most satisfactory for your work. I personally always use a clear glue which can be applied straight from the tube.

Bostik adhesive is excellent as it is both clear and can be used straight from the tube with little mess and practically no waste. Bostik also gives a strong bond which lasts for years. If you should happen to get any unwanted Bostik on your background, it can be removed whilst it is still damp with a fine pointed object. With other glues this is virtually impossible. Drying time for this adhesive is considerably less than with an epoxy resin glue — approximately 10 minutes — giving you time to adhere several layers of shell petals and reach an end product quickly and efficiently.

Evo-Stik is another adhesive to be considered in work with shells. This adhesive must be left to go 'tacky', and it must be remembered that it is a contact adhesive, so there is very little chance to alter the position of the shell once pressure has been applied. It is, however, very good for securing the background material to the hardboard backing of your shell picture.

Epoxy resin adhesives, such as Araldite, give a very strong bond, but as these have to be carefully mixed and take several hours to set, they are not really suitable, being time consuming and messy.

With all adhesives it must be remembered that the application of either too much or too little will result in either a messy, unprofessional appearance to the picture, or the failure of the shells to adhere.

When applying adhesive to very small shells I hold them with tweezers in one hand and, with the other, apply the glue to the shell by means of a sharpened matchstick or cocktail stick. Care must be taken not to trail glue across your background while putting the shells into position.

While you are laying out your picture, Blu-tack is very useful for holding the shells temporarily in place and it does not mark or stain the shells or background.

A selection of useful shells and equipment

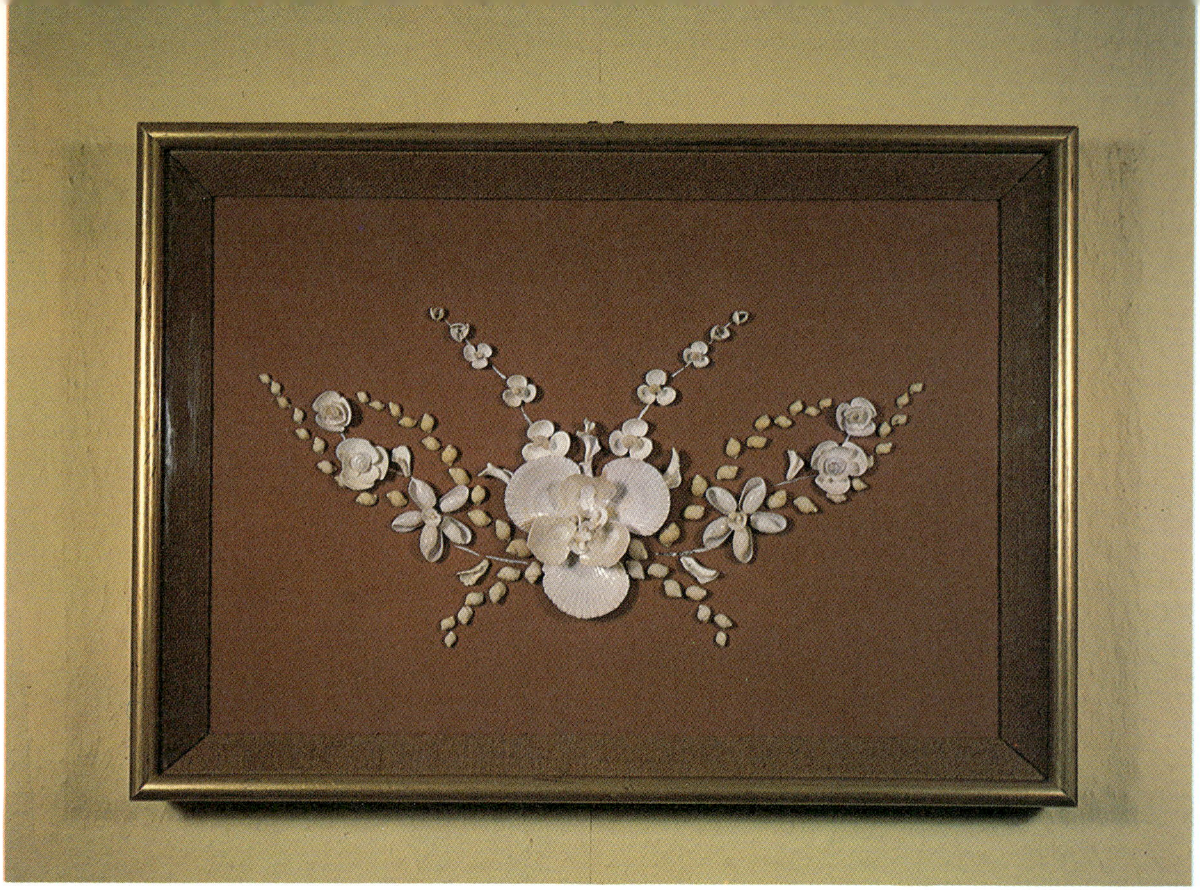

Above: plate 4 *Below: plate 5*

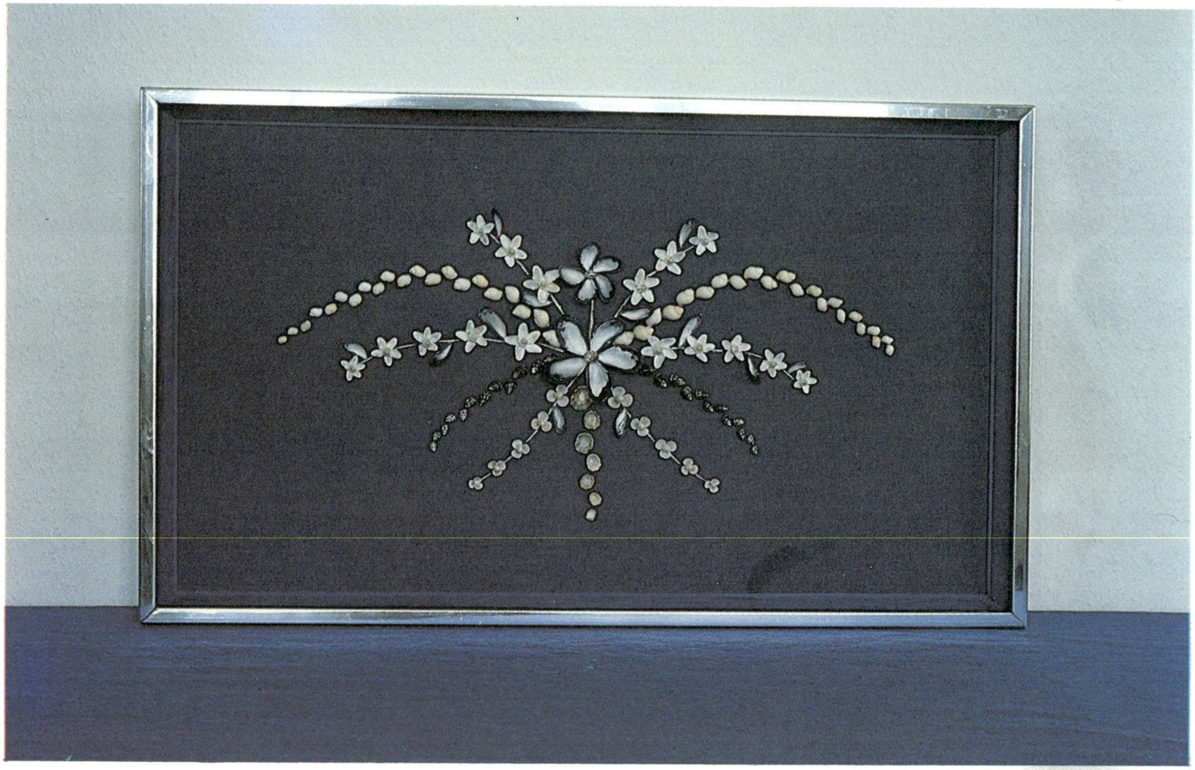

Plate 6

Backgrounds

The first thing is to decide upon the type of picture you wish to make, as this will determine the weight of the background needed. For a large picture you will need something rigid, such as hardboard, but do not use plywood as this is too heavy and you will find it difficult to support. For something smaller, where less rigidity is needed, use cardboard.

All manner of materials can be used for backgrounds; hardboard, cardboard and natural pine are among the best and most versatile as they can be left natural, painted or covered with a strong fabric. They are all relatively inexpensive and give a good textured surface on which to work.

Hardboard is a particularly useful background. It can be left natural, especially if you buy the 'sandy' coloured board, and you have the option of using either the textured or the smooth surface. It can be painted with any household paint and the textured paints now available can be extremely effective. Hardboard is ideal for large designs, because it is very rigid, but not too heavy.

Another good material for backgrounds is natural wood, especially pine, as it is fairly inexpensive and easy to obtain. Pine usually contains interesting grains and knots, and dark shells are well set-off by this background, especially if the natural grains of the wood are used to enhance the shells. An added advantage of using natural wood is that a frame is not necessary as the wood can be used to take the hanging screws. However, the edges must be sandpapered smooth before you begin your picture.

The addition of one or two coats of clear, polyurethane varnish will give your natural wood background a pleasing finish and also act as a sealer. You can buy either matt or gloss varnish. There are, however, several woods which will not take being sealed, so always ask if there are any manufacturer's recommendations when you purchase your materials. Wood can also of course be painted with a household paint.

All the aforementioned backgrounds can also be covered with a fabric such as hessian, strong cotton, felt, velvet or linen. Most materials should only be glued to smaller backgrounds, as it is very difficult to stretch the material really taut over a large area, and it is important to have a tight background on which to work. Otherwise, the weight of your shells will make the material separate from the background and sag. Materials such as felt, however, can be glued very successfully, as it has no open weave to fray apart. I find that Evostick or Araldite are best for this purpose. Allow 7.5cm (3in) for your turnings.

When dealing with large areas it is best to cover the backing board by sewing the material firmly across the back with strong thread. First, lay your background board on the wrong side of the material, making sure the edges of the board are along the straight grain of the weave. Next, draw your cutting line, allowing approximately three inches all around the board, for your turnings. Using a strong, button thread, sew the two opposite edges of material together as in figure 8, keeping the thread as taut as possible. When complete, fasten the thread off securely. Turn the board around and fold the other two opposite edges in, taking care to mitre the corners figure 9. Continue by sewing the opposite edges together in the same manner as before figure 10. When the thread needs joining, join it with a very strong knot. This saves continual casting on and off. When the design has been finished, the backboard may be neatened by gluing thick brown paper over the sewing.

Paper may be used to cover cardboard, but it does tend to stretch and buckle when glued, especially if a light weight paper is used.

Figure 8.   9.   10.
Background stretching.

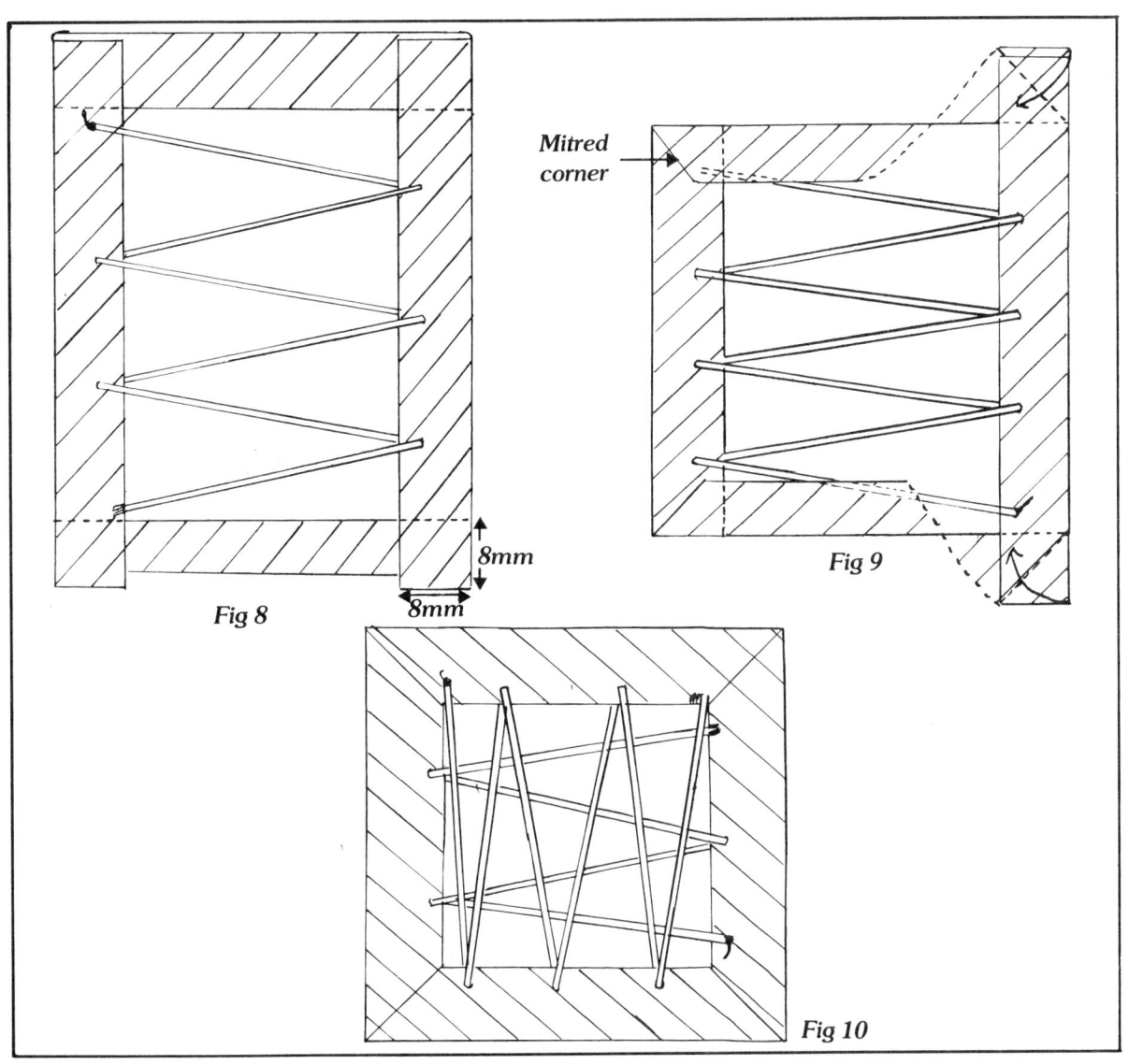

Mitred
corner

8mm

8mm

Fig 8

Fig 9

Fig 10

Therefore, I find it best to buy ready coloured mounting board. If a more rigid background is required then glue the mounting board to a piece of hardboard. Mounting board is available in a large variety of colours and can be bought from any art shop.

Cork, glass, linoleum, putty and earthenware are also good background materials. Cork tiles can be glued to a hardboard backing, giving an interesting, textured appearance. Linoleum may be used in the same manner.

Glass is a good background on which to mount shells. Glass bottles can either have shells glued straight on to them, examples of which will be found in this book, or they may be covered first with putty and then the shells arranged in the putty.

Cork tiles make attractive backgrounds.

Never mount shells in wet clay, as when the clay dries it shrinks and pushes them out. Plastics and polystyrene also make poor backgrounds as most adhesives damage or dissolve these materials.

A very important fact to remember when choosing a background, is the colour. I find that natural colours display shells to the best advantage such as dark greens, browns, beiges, sandy colours and blues. Other colours can also be very successful, if the colour of the shells is taken into account.

The background can either contrast or tone. For example, a blue could be used as a background, with mauve to white shells to tone in, or a red background with white shells to contrast. Always remember that texture is also an essential factor in your background choice.

Types of useful shells

As you work with shells, you will undoubtedly find that the most useful shells in your collection are those which are regular shapes; round, oval, wedge, pointed or oblong. These are always a good stand-by to use as a background cover.

Some useful shell types are Limpets, Tellins, Nerites, Bubble shells, Augers, Pearly Trochuses, Scallops and Cowries. See plate 1.

Colours and patterns

The basic colours and patterns of shells are inherited genetically, but of course there are many natural variations as in the hair and skin colouring of human beings.

Environment and diet has a profound effect on the colouration of shells. Sunlight and warmth are essential to the bright and varied colours which are, in some cases, a built-in camouflage. The shells of molluscs which live in warm waters are usually more colourful than those of molluscs from cold waters.

Some molluscs have developed extraordinary shaped shells either as camouflage for protection or to enable them to live in areas and surroundings that others cannot inhabit.

There are four characteristics to look for when choosing shells for a working collection; size, colour, shape and texture.

Chapter 3

A SIMPLE BEGINNING

Learning the basics of a new craft or art is rather like starting a new adventure, one just does not know what is in store. So it is always wise to have a basic knowledge of the craft and the materials available before tackling any large projects.

This chapter is aimed at showing you how some of the simpler pieces can be made. The projects covered may be simple, but they give pleasing results and valuable experience will be gained whilst you are working on them. Shellcraft is quite easy in that there are no stitches or specialised terms to learn. It is similar to painting in that it is completely individual and works well as long as your design is balanced and the colour harmonies are good.

In this chapter you also will find some helpful hints and tips on shellcraft. Shells lend themselves very well to flower patterns and there are details on this in the following pages.

Working with shells

Working with shells can be rewarding and satisfying as well as great fun. Their natural colours and shapes make them a marvellous medium in which to work. They are also extremely versatile because they not only adhere to each other, but also to many other materials. Shells also work well with other natural forms such as pebbles, coral, seaweed, dried ferns and grasses. These are useful as flower stems or leaves and can provide light relief from shells.

Always use perfect shells in your designs, unless of course broken ones are particularly required, but shells that have been slightly damaged or chipped can spoil the whole effect.

Some people like to paint, stain or even varnish the shells they use, but I personally think this is criminal as they are so beautiful and colourful in their own right. If used with imagination and care you should find shells suitable for most of your design requirements.

Shells adhere quickly and easily to most surfaces and, as very little adhesive is needed, it is a good idea to apply glue to the shell with a cocktail stick or matchstick.

As each shell is different in some way, it is almost impossible to make two pictures alike, thus total originality is maintained.

Larger shells, such as the Great Scallop, are usually discarded, or else used as ash trays, because they are generally considered too big and clumsy for this particular craft, but when looked at closely they will be seen to be very attractive shells.

Needle case

Here, two of these pretty Scallops have been used as a needle case. The shells, decorated with lace and ribbon, have been transformed into attractive and extremely useful objects. They make super gifts and you will be able to obtain the shells quite easily and cheaply from your local fishmonger.

You will need

2 matching Scallop shells
1 felt square 22cm × 22cm (9in × 9in)
0.5m (18in) lace
0.5m (18in) ribbon 6mm (0.25in) wide
Clear adhesive
High speed steel twist drill, sized 3/16in.

Step 1

Choose your decorations to tone with the colour shells. In this particular example brown and beige were used.

Needle cases made from Scallop shells.

Place one of the shells on the felt and draw around its perimeter. Cut out the shapes just inside the pencil line, so they are just a little smaller than the shell itself. Three pieces should be adequate. Holding the three pieces together, stitch along the straight edge at the top. Pinking shears can be used to make a decorative edging.

Step 2

Next, drill two holes in the hinged edges of both shells and make two corresponding holes through the three pieces of felt. Shells are easy to drill. All you need is a small diameter drill bit. Let the drill push its own way through the shell, being careful not to apply too much pressure, which could cause the shell to shatter. Thread the ribbon through the holes in the shells and felt in a criss cross fashion and tie into a bow at the front. See figure 11.

Step 3

Drill another hole in the front of each shell, approximately 1cm (0.5in) from the bottom edge, making sure that they match. Then, tie a length of ribbon through the holes of both shells. Finish off by gluing the lace around the inside edge of the bottom shell. See figure 12. Beige lace was used to contrast with the brown ribbon and felt.

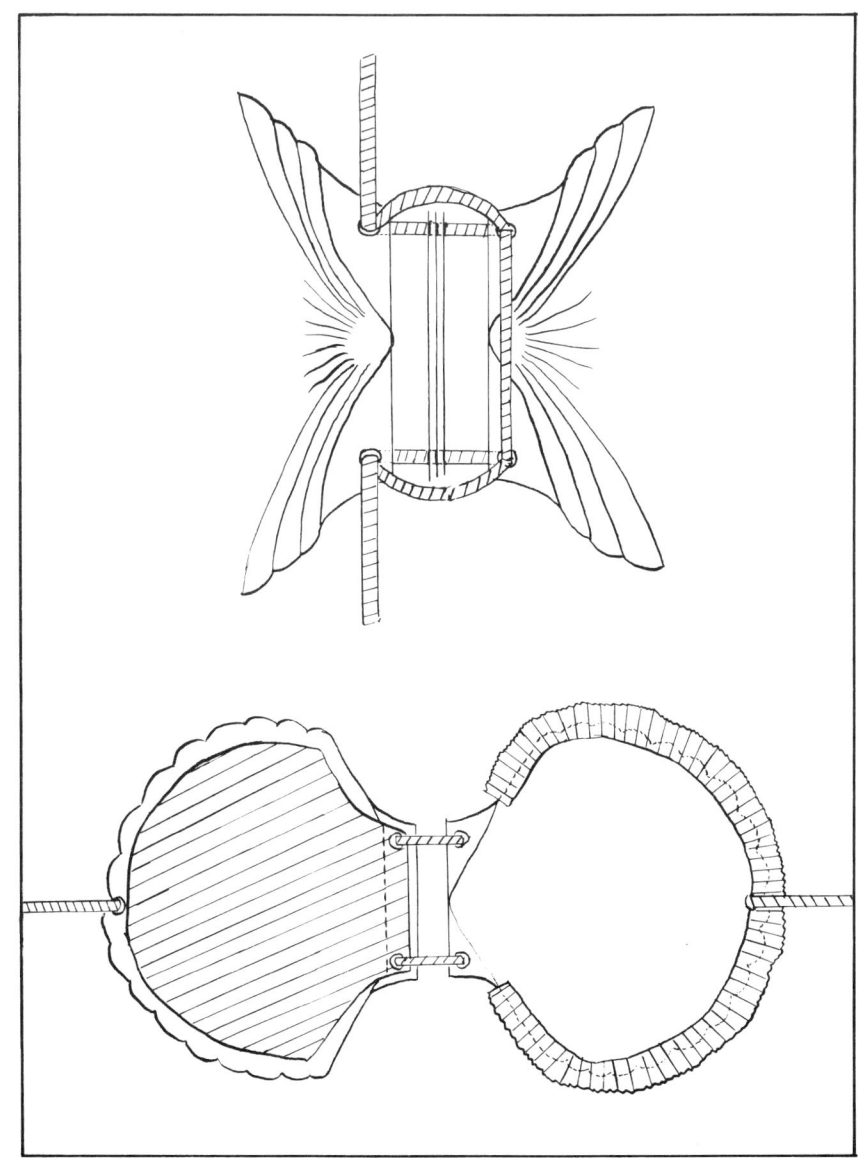

Figure 11.
Threading the ribbon in a criss cross fashion.

Figure 12.
The felt leaves and lace around inner edge of the shell.

Shell mobile

Another way of using shells which are too large for a shell design, is to make a shell mobile. Once the holes have been drilled in each shell, a young child can quite easily make the mobile with little or no help from an adult.

You will need

Nylon fishing line
1 10cm (4in) rush table mat
Assorted sea shells
High speed steel twist drill, sized 3/32in.
Stapler

Step 1

First choose your shells. The shells used in the example are Dove Shells, Umbonium, Smooth Cockles, Common Cockles and Scallops. Drill a small hole in the top of each shell for the nylon thread.

Step 2

Thread the shells onto lengths of nylon using a knot to stop them from slipping. Try to vary the lengths of nylon and the position of the shells. The number of lengths used is entirely a personal preference — in this example I have used six.

Step 3

Now that you have all the shells threaded onto lengths of nylon, staple the nylon to the top of the rush mat, using a stapler, allowing the nylon to hang over the edge of the mat. Finish off by attaching a piece of nylon to the centre of the mat from which to hang the mobile.

Miniature shell display 25cm × 45cm (9.75in × 17.75in)

This is an interesting way of displaying individual shells from your collection when you do not have enough of certain types to make a shell design. See photograph on page 38.

Blue hessian was chosen for this design because it shows the colours, shapes and textures of the shells off to their best advantage.

When making a display of this kind, try to use a few larger shells to add height and depth to the picture. As the correct use of colour can help balance the picture, be careful to harmonise the colours of the shells and make sure that none clash.

The frame was a wood moulding with an antique finish. The gold in the picture frame picks out the yellow and orange in the shells and, being a medium sized moulding, it gives the picture width and draws the eye down into the design.

Shell mobile.

Miniature shell display

Holders

Below: tall jars

Altogether I have used 33 shells in this display and they are of all colours and sizes, ranging from 6mm (0.25in) to 4.7cm (1.75in). Remember with a design of this size that it can be temporarily laid out before the final gluing.

Key to Miniature shell display showing the 33 shell types.

1. CLUB URCHIN SPINE
2. ROSE PETAL
3. CERITHIUM
4. COMMON BLUE MUSSEL
5. WENTLETRAP
6. COMMON COCKLE
7. OLIVE SHELL
8. TORTOISESHELL LIMPET
9. LAND SNAIL
10. CONE
11. NUT SHELL
12. LUCINA SHELL
13. VIRGIN NERITE
14. VARIEGATED SCALLOP
15. WEST INDIAN BUBBLE SHELL
16. ROUGH WINKLE
17. PINK BALTIC TELLIN
18. TUSK SHELL
19. LIMPET
20. GOLD RINGER COWRIE
21. VARIEGATED NERITE
22. YELLOW BALTIC TELLIN
23. VENUS SHELL
24. ROUGH LIMPET
25. WHITE SPOTTED ENGINA
26. ATLANTIC SLIPPER SHELL
27. BANDED WEDGE SHELL
28. FLAT WINKLE
29. BUBBLE SHELL
30. SPECTRAL CONE
31. MICRODON COWRIE
32. COFFEE BEAN SHELL
33. HORN SHELL

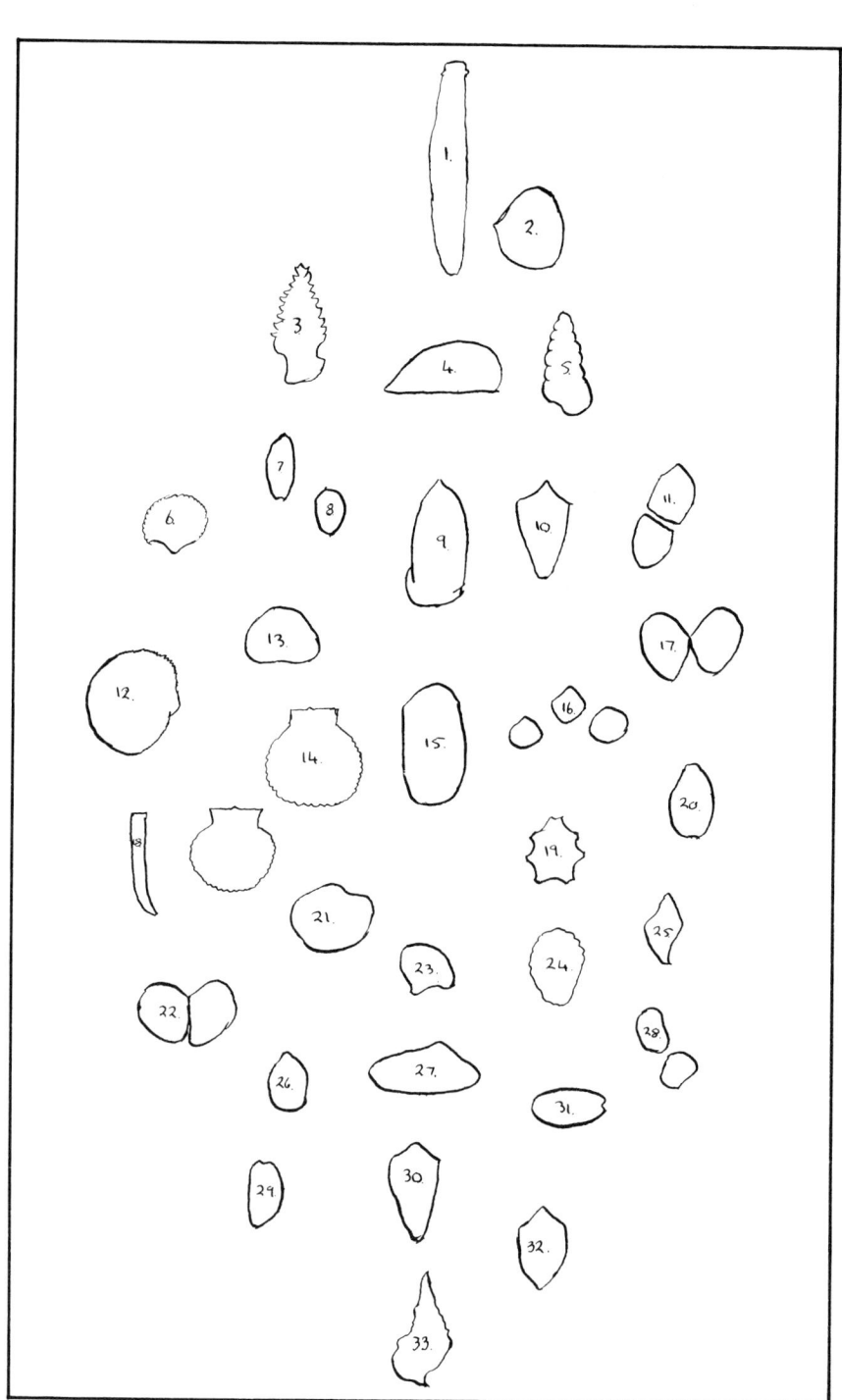

Covering up Plate 2

Another attractive, but easy way to display shells is to use them to cover and decorate bottles, jars, boxes or any other suitable objects. These pretty little knick-knacks can be used as cigarette holders, paperweights, bedside lamps or even just ornaments.

Almost all this type of work should be carried out with tweezers and a cocktail stick because the shells used are too small and delicate to handle with your fingers.

First in this section are glass jars. As they are made from rather attractive glass, the amount of shells used is quite negligible and they have been arranged in simple and very open patterns so that the colour of the glass may be seen.

Blue jar

Only three types of shell were used to decorate this jar, enabling the pattern to be kept quite simple. The shells used are Pearly Trochuses, Dove Shells and Rose Petal Shells. These particular shells are ideal for this type of work because they are of a uniform shape, small and easily obtainable in large quantities. When covering jars, you will find it is easier to form a pattern if you start by covering the base. In this case a ring of Trochuses were used.

A selection of covered jars and bottles.

Brown jar

The pattern on this jar was formed by first putting a ring of Dove Shells around the base. I decided this pattern should have a centre-piece and so this was applied next. It is easier to glue the shells if the jar is placed upon its side. This can be done either by securing the jar in a small container of sand or by holding it in place with Blu-tack and leaving it in this position until the glue has dried. After the centre-piece has been completed, the rest of the design can then be carried out. This particular centre-piece was made up of Planaxis Shells and Striped Umboniums.

Pearly Trochuses, Dove Shells and Umboniums were used to make the overall pattern. A few simple flowers made from Rose Petal Shells have also been added.

Holders Photograph on page 39, top

The examples in this photograph have been decorated for use as cocktail stick holders. One has been completely covered with shells, again starting at the bottom and working upwards, using the shells to form a banded pattern. Only three types of shells were used to achieve this effect, Rose Petals, Pearly Trochuses and Prickly Cockle Shells.

On the second jar a more open pattern has been used. As the jar is made from clear perspex I decided to use shells that were of a pale colour so as to keep the whole effect light in tone. Among the shells used are Trochuses, Rose Petals, Dove Shells, Tusk Shells, Top Shells and, to give a contrast, a centre-piece of Planaxis Shells.

Tall jars

In the bottom photograph on page 39 are examples of slightly more complicated patterns, giving completely different effects.

Two of the jars have been decorated with a panelled pattern. This was achieved by first gluing a ring of Pearly Trochuse Shells around the base, then a similar ring around the neck. Next four vertical lines, equal distances apart, were made from Rose Petal Shells. The panels in between these lines were then filled alternately with Trochuses and small Rose Petal Shells. To finish off, Prickly Cockle Shells and tiny Rose Petal Shells were used around the top.

On the next jar, shells were used to create a completely different pattern. Again the pattern was started at the base using black Planaxis and then a ring of Umbonium shells, so giving a sturdy appearance to the base of the jar. A ring of Nerites was then applied just above the neck of the jar.

The twisting movement was the next step and this is done by using Pearly Trochuses and Rose Petals in alternate rows at a 60° angle. The pattern was finished off with a row of Cockle Shells and filled in between with tiny Rose Petal Shells. The effect is similar to that of a Roman architectural column.

Powder compact

Upon most bedroom dressing-tables a powder compact will be found. Some are very attractive, whilst others may be very plain, so why not decorate your own? Here is an example of a transformed powder compact.

This pattern was started from the outside with three rings of Pearly Trochuse Shells. These particular shells were used here because this part of the compact would receive pressure when being opened and Trochuses are quite tough.

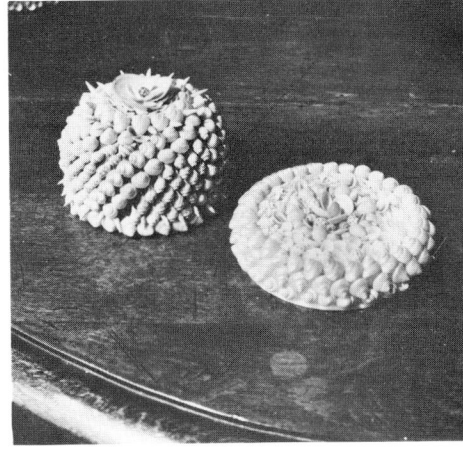

Powder compact and paperweight

When the rings of shells were dry, the centre of the compact top was found by measuring, then, a small flower of Nut Shells applied. Dove Shells were then placed around the flower to keep the circular effect. From the line of Dove Shells, Spotted Cowries and Top Shells were added in radiating lines and, to complete the design, Rose Petal Shells were used as a background filler. The result is a very attractive gift.

Paperweight

This paperweight was made from the plastic top of an aerosol can. First, the top was filled with Polyfilla as this gives the top its necessary weight. When the Polyfilla has completely dried, sand it until smooth and then cover the bottom with felt.

Next, put a ring of sturdy shells around the bottom, pearly Trochuse shells were used. On this particular paperweight. Three Baltic Tellins, three Nut Shells and a Nerite combine to make the flower centre-piece. The remainder of the top has been decorated with angled panels of Trochuses and Dove Shells.

Bedside lamp Photograph on page 41

Wine bottles are often turned into lamps after being filled with marbles, covered with melted candle wax or else covered with putty into which shells are then pushed and varnished. However, such lamps usually have a rather clumsy, amateurish appearance.

Here is an example of a wine bottle which has been decorated with shells, but they have been used very sparingly. Small, delicate flowers were made from Rose Petal Shells and trailing stems of Umbonium and Slipper Shells complete the dainty effect. To give a sturdy base, both for practicability and effectiveness, a row of dark Cockle shells have also been used.

Flower making

When making flowers of any type or number always use shells that match in size and colour, unless of course you are making a stem of graduating flowers. A daisy, for example, can be made from any number of shells, but they must be of equal size. The quantity is something of a personal choice or can be determined by the amount of equally sized shells available.

Making shells into flower forms is probably one of the more simple and obvious ways of using shells. Their shape and colour, in many cases, resemble flower petals or they can even give the effect of an already complete flower. See pages 46 and 47.

They can be used to represent real flowers such as daisies or roses, or to make imaginary flowers. Single flowers or blooms that only have one ring or whorl of petals are the best to start with as they are easier to make and do not require a large amount of shells.

In Fig. (a) you will see how simple a single daisy is, but a small group or spray of daisies can also be extremely effective. This particular daisy was made from eight small Banded Wedge Shells. These were glued into position with a small amount of glue on the very tip of the shell, and then held in place by propping up the individual petals with pebbles until dry and secure. In the centre is a Rough Winkle Shell. They are particularly good for this purpose because of their uniform shape. Winkles, Nerites, Tusk Shells, Snails, small Whelks and many more of similar shapes also make effective flower centres. They can also be used as the spikes, panicle or plumes of flowers.

When used in this manner the shells must graduate in size, starting at the bottom of the stem with largest shells you intend to use, as in Fig. (b), and gradually working your way along the stem using smaller and smaller shells until finally finishing with the smallest shells which may represent a bud.

Making double flowers, where the bloom may have two or more rings of petals, calls for a little more time and patience and a large supply of shells. The shell-petal layers must of course diminish in size as they come nearer the centre. A good example of this is the rose. In Fig. (c), Baltic Tellins have been used to demonstrate how the number of shells used in a particular flower can completely alter the effect. One rose was made from nine shells, so giving a full, double bloom, whilst in the other, only three were used making it a simpler, single flower.

The rose bud was made from four shells, also Baltic Tellins, but there are numerous other shells that are suitable. This time the shells were used with the blunt end secured to the background, so directing the pointed end upwards. Again you will see how well Nerites and Turret Shells act as flower centres.

Always have a few pebbles or larger shells near to hand when making flowers because they can be used to hold your shells in position while the adhesive dries as in Fig. (d). Blu-tack can also be used for this purpose.

Fig. (e) shows just a small number of flower examples which can be made with the more abundant shells. There is no limit to the variety that can be achieved with a little time, patience and imagination.

Flower stems often benefit from the addition of a few leaves, and some shells seem to lend themselves readily to this; Mussell Shells, Ark Shells and Pen Shells. Broken Razor Shells make good fine stems for flowers, but sometimes another material will seem better, such as dried seaweed or fern, but whichever material is used it should be fine.

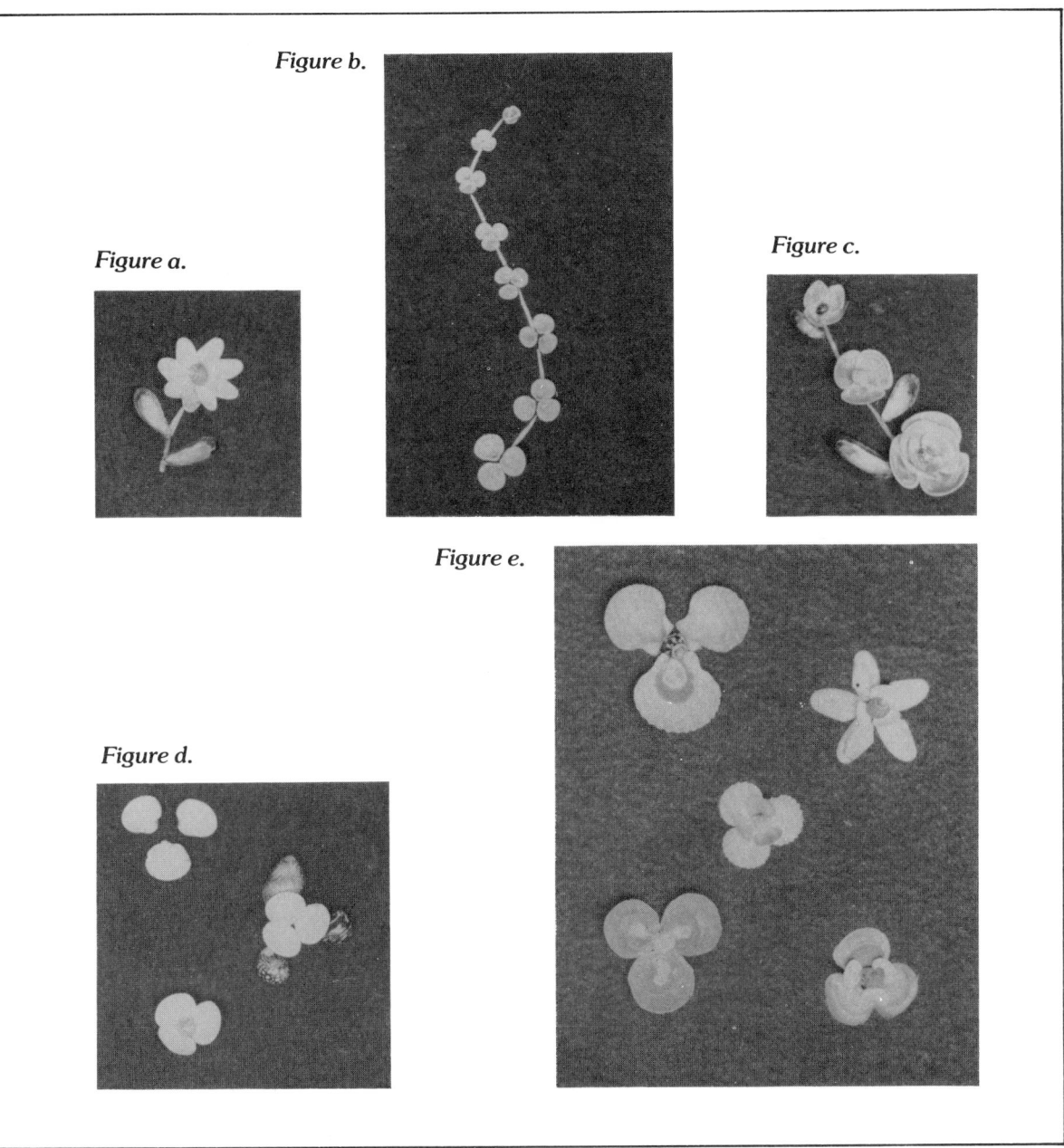

Figure a.

Figure b.

Figure c.

Figure d.

Figure e.

Placing the shell. Small stones holding the shells in position.

Applying glue to the shell.

46

Placing centre shell using tweezers.

Placing mussell shell 'leaves.'

47

Green wall hanging 11cm × 45cm (4.5in × 18in)

The small picture in the photograph below is an ideal first project as it uses very few shells and is inexpensive being simply framed with upholstery braid. The background material is green felt which needs no stitching as it can be glued onto cardboard. As this is only a small picture it is better to keep the arrangement simple and use small shells.

Start the picture with the largest flower you intend to use, arrange it on the background and glue it. Then proceed to lay out the other shell flowers graduating them in size as previously explained. Always remember to keep movement in the design. The flowers in this particular picture are all made from white Cockle shells, with grey-black Nerites in the centre. To add a little colour and to balance the shape of the picture, greenish Limpet shells were also used.

As the picture is quite small, dried fern was used for foliage because shells would have looked too heavy and clumsy. All the work in this picture can be carried out with very few tools — just glue, tweezers and nimble fingers.

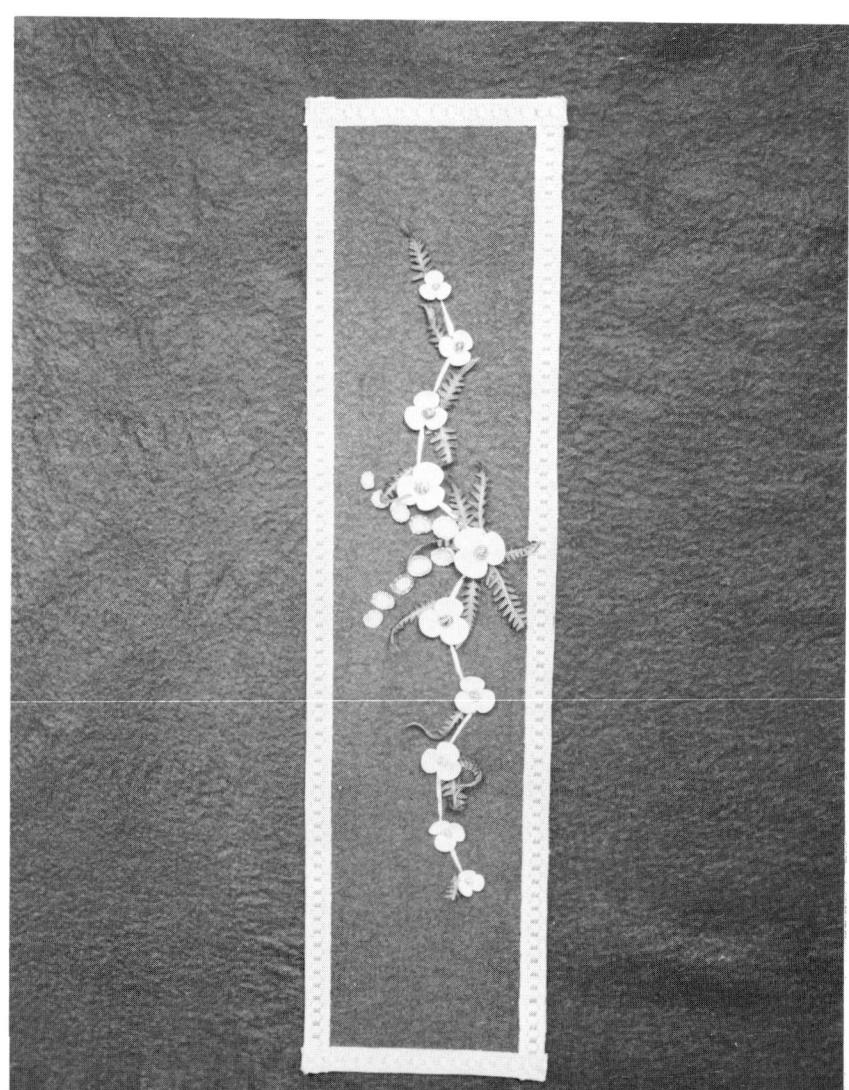

Chapter 4

PRETTY AS A PICTURE

Being one of the earth's oldest inhabitants, dating back millions of years, molluscs have evolved into one of nature's most beautiful, varied and in some cases precious creations. Their need for camouflage in order to survive in the waters of the world has caused them to become varied in shape and colour. Some are brightly camouflaged so as to become lost in the colourful world of the coral reefs, and others have become drab and strangely shaped so as not to be seen among the rocks of colder seas.

Because they are so varied and easy to acquire shells have always been very popular with man. The Egyptians were the first race to use them in the form of pictures as far as we know. They used thousands of shells to make elaborate murals on the walls of their burial chambers.

The Victorians used them to make large, shell-encrusted ornate, pictures. These pictures became so enormous that they had to be housed in box frames, which were sometimes 15cm (6in) deep.

In this chapter you will find examples of shell pictures and designs made for the homes of today and I hope that they will serve as inspiration to the reader.

Planning your design

First, decide upon the type of picture you wish to make and then choose a suitable background material. Remember to take into account the texture and colour which will be most beneficial to your design.

A book alone cannot teach people how to design because there are no hard and fast rules and every individual has personal likes and dislikes. You can really only learn from experience and trial and error.

Some readers may find that it helps to have an idea of the design you are aiming at, in which case it is best to draw out a small plan from which you can work; others may like to work out the design as you go along; but whichever method is chosen always be prepared to adapt the design according to the colours and shapes of the shells available.

Shells must be chosen carefully for colour, shape and texture.

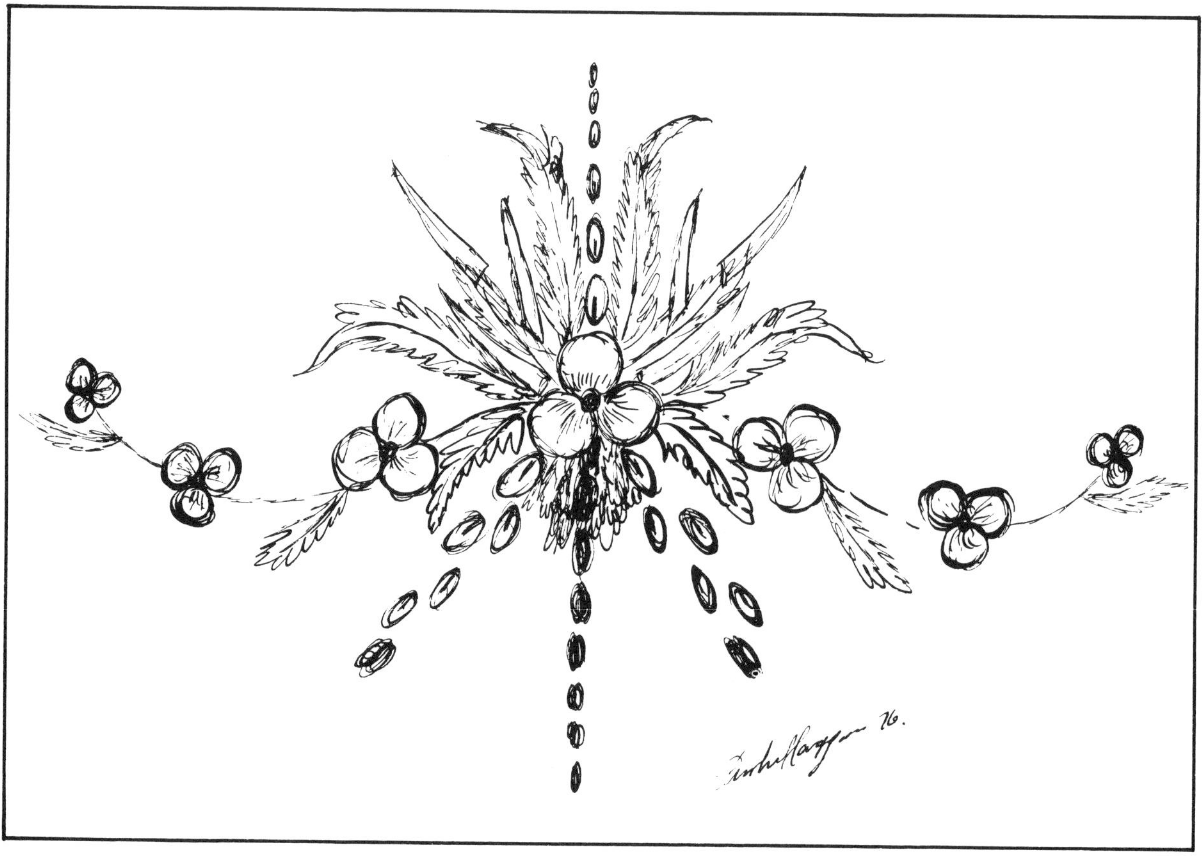

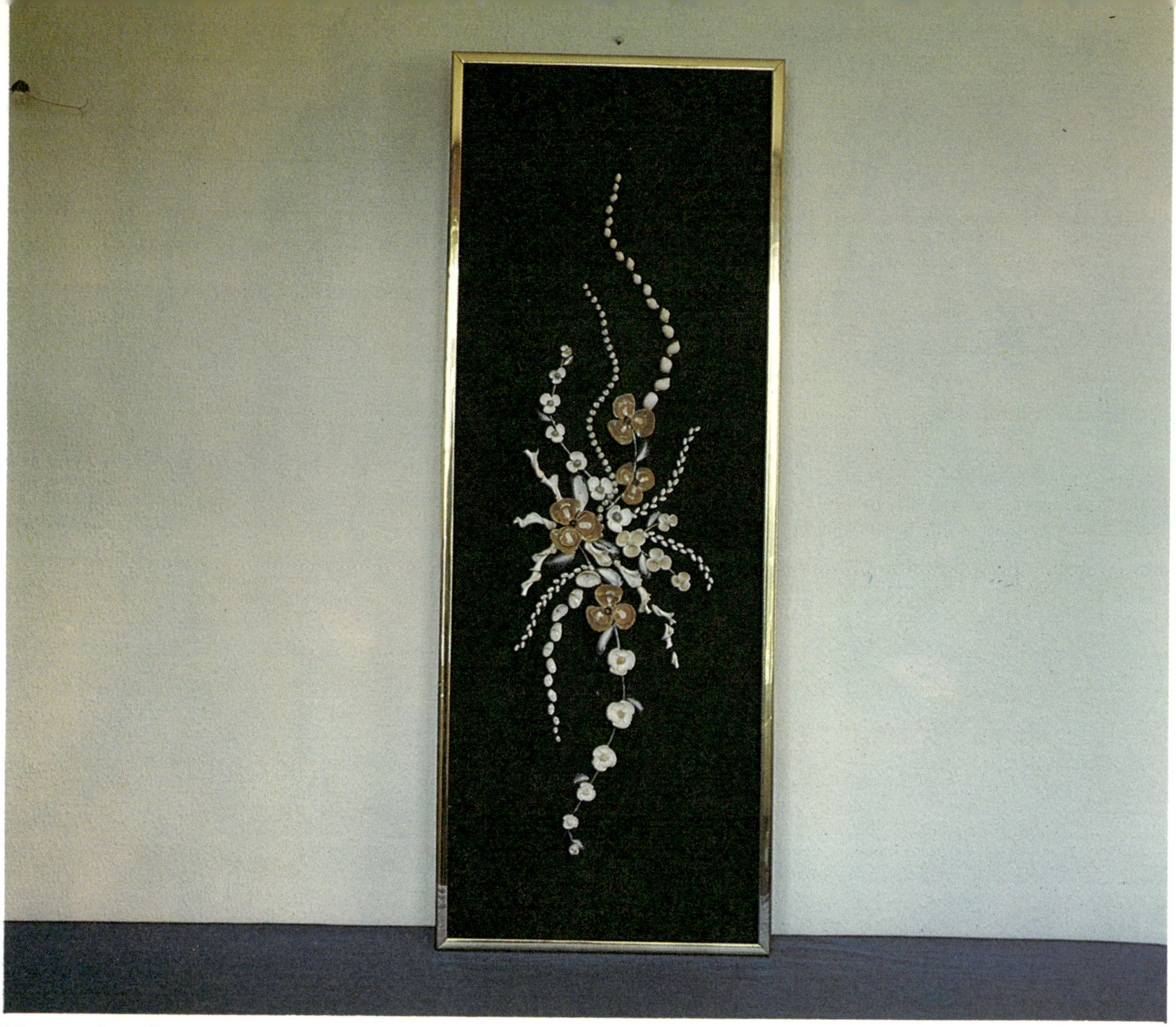

Above: plate 7

Below: plate 8

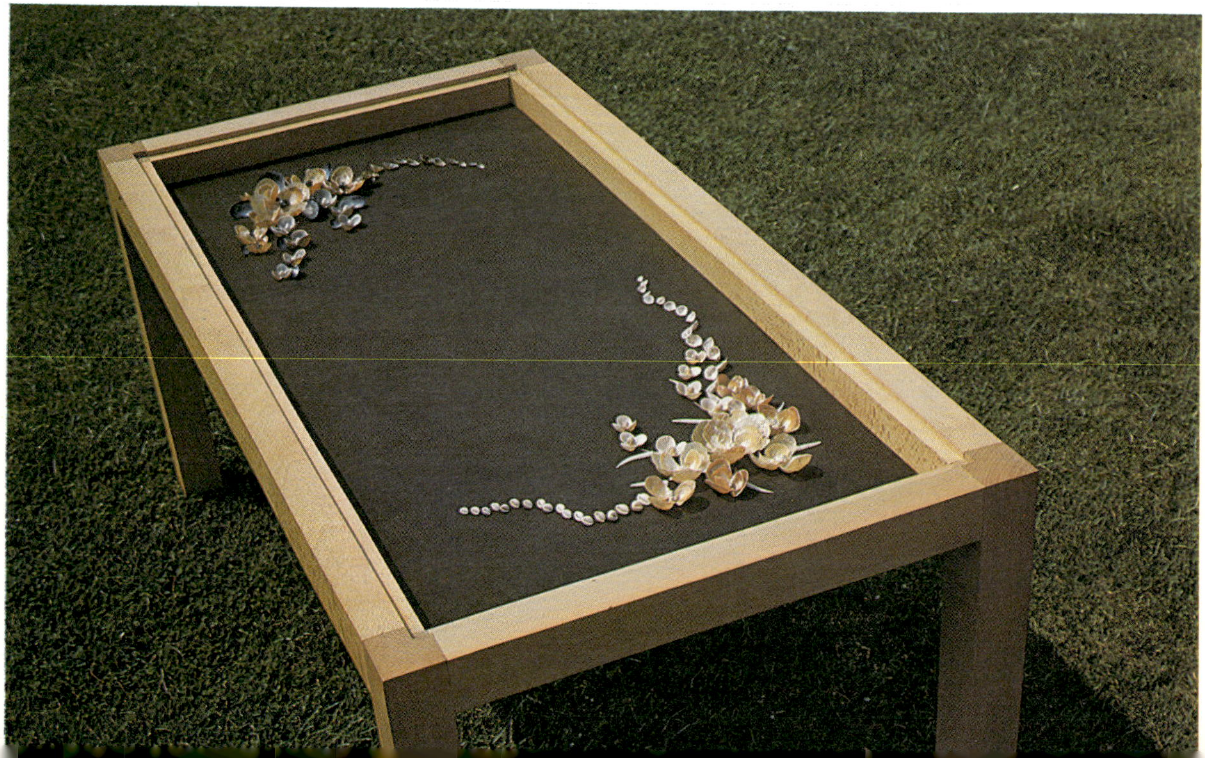

Plate 9

Always be on the look out for poor colour combinations as they can spoil your picture. Here, it is a matter of personal taste. What may be pleasing to one person is displeasing to another.

Only arrange small areas of your design at a time. Place the shells on the background and move them around until you are pleased with the effect. You can hold them in position temporarily with Blu-tack or small pebbles, but never glue your shells until you are completely satisfied with the arrangement. Do not try to lay out the whole design before gluing permanently as you will find it becomes more and more difficult to work and you will not be able to lift and glue the shells that are in the centre of the design. There is also the possibility that your design will be jogged and the shells will be knocked out of position. This can be very frustrating.

I try never to use damaged or discoloured shells in designs because nothing is worse than a wonderful flower which has had chipped or cracked shells in it. Therefore, always try to use perfect specimens. However, gastropods that have been pounded by the sea can be beautiful shapes and may be a useful asset to your picture, especially in abstract designs.

Never try to include too many shells, otherwise it will become overcrowded and jumbled and you will lose all balance and harmony.

Frames

Framing is a very important stage, because it will either add or detract from your picture.

There are several alternatives open to you as regards framing:

1) Special frame made to fit.
2) Ready made frame kit.
3) Existing old frame.
4) Make your own.
5) To mount subject material on unframed wood.

Having a frame made professionally for your picture is the easiest and usually the most successful, but this can be expensive and there is normally a delay of about two weeks between ordering and collecting the frame.

Ready made frame kits are a good alternative as they are very easily assembled and can be obtained from most art shops. Remember when making your picture, if you intend to use a frame kit, that they are only available in a limited range of sizes. So, either make a note of the various sizes available, or buy the frame first and make your picture to fit.

Buying a second-hand frame and making the picture to fit can also be a very successful alternative. Oval, round and hand-carved frames are almost impossible to have made now, but you can usually find

them in second-hand shops, jumble sales, or auction rooms. When purchasing you may find that you also have to buy the usually non-descript picture already in the frame, but this should not increase the price too much and by comparison to other framing methods it is quite cheap.

Make sure when buying a second-hand frame that it is not falling apart, as it would need a professional to repair it. It may of course need cleaning but this is quite an easy task — just wash with warm water. Some attractive wood frames may have been painted or varnished. This can be stripped off with a liquid paint stripper and then the frame can be stained, repainted or left natural after a protective coating of polyurethane has been applied.

Should you be lucky enough to obtain a gilt frame, then just clean it with a dry cloth, but never use water as this is prone to take the gilt off. If the frame should begin to lose its gilt then you can cheer it up by giving it an application of liquid or wax gilt. This again can be bought from most art shops.

Making your own frame can be an absolute disaster if you have never worked with wood before and do not possess the necessary tools and equipment. If, however, you do have the tools, have a go and you may find it is not really too difficult to master. Lengths of frame moulding can be bought from most handicraft or art shops. It is important to be extremely accurate with your measurements otherwise the mitred corners will be untidy. It is quite a delicate process and can be very costly in wasted materials.

If you want to learn this craft, then you will find the details in most do-it-yourself woodwork books. A mitre machine is very useful for producing perfect mitres, but they are expensive.

If you prefer to make the picture on a board of natural wood you will not need a frame as you can screw the hanging hooks straight into the wood.

Restraint in your design

When I first started designing with shells I had an overwhelming desire to try and cover the whole background and put almost everything I could think of in the picture. Overcrowding a picture made with shells is very easily done, by just adding a rose here or small spray of daisies there, and the whole thing can quickly become a complete mess.

Knowing the point at which to stop will come with experience and I have given two examples of simple designs using only a few shells and leaving a considerable area of open background, thus giving the light, airy effect which I feel one should try to achieve.

Flower collage 38cm × 18cm (14in × 7in)

The composition in the photograph on page 58 shows how effectively a balanced design can be created using only a small amount of carefully chosen shells. A light brown suedette material mounted on hardboard has been used for the background. The design was started by putting on the beige Prickly Cockle Shells and white Venus Shell flowers. From this, the long, waving sprays of black Planaxis work their way outwards giving height and width to the picture.

The other shells involved are a spray of Coffee Bean Shells, Blue Mussel Shells and broken gastropods form the leaves. Black Nerites and yellow flat Snail Shells serve as flower centres and the composition is completed with a pretty pink butterfly made from a Thin Tellin Shell.

The entire collage was framed in a stained, natural wood with a small gold fillet which helps to bring out the brown and beige, otherwise dormant, in the shells.

Blue collage 43cm × 24cm (17in × 10in)

The colour content of the small collage in the photograph on page 59 is quite varied, but note that the colours enhance one another and do not clash. The three larger flowers are made from nine stunning yellow and pink Baltic Tellins (which are of completely natural colouring).

Small Rose Petal Shells make pretty flower sprays which wind their way out from the centre. The Dove Shells have been used in an attractive way, by placing four with the blunt ends together — the effect is a star shaped flower.

Umbonium, Black Planaxis and Rice shells have made pretty trails of colour through the picture from the centre which gives the feeling of width and length.

The design has been framed in stainless steel, with a blue fillet making the design appear wider.

Flower collage

Opposite: Blue collage

Plate 10

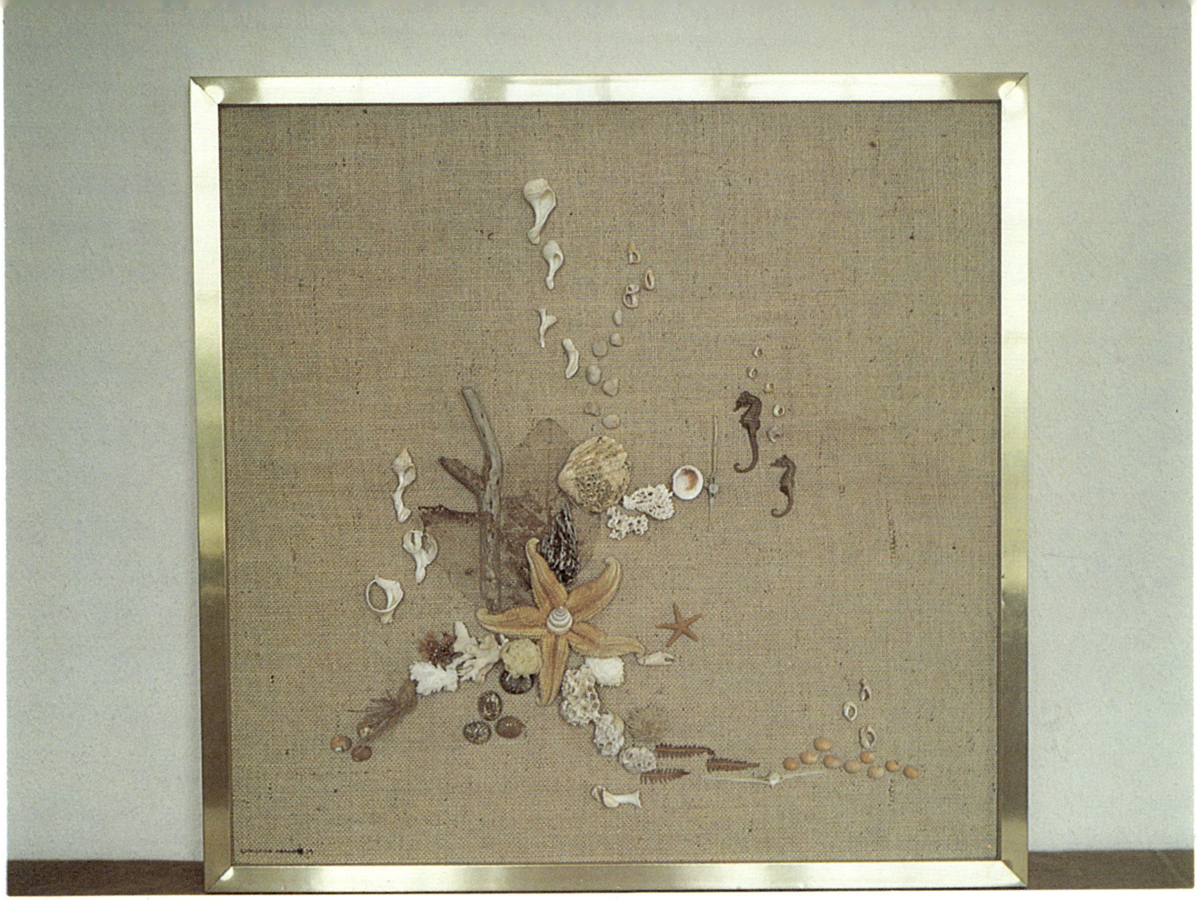

Above: plate 11

Below: plate 12

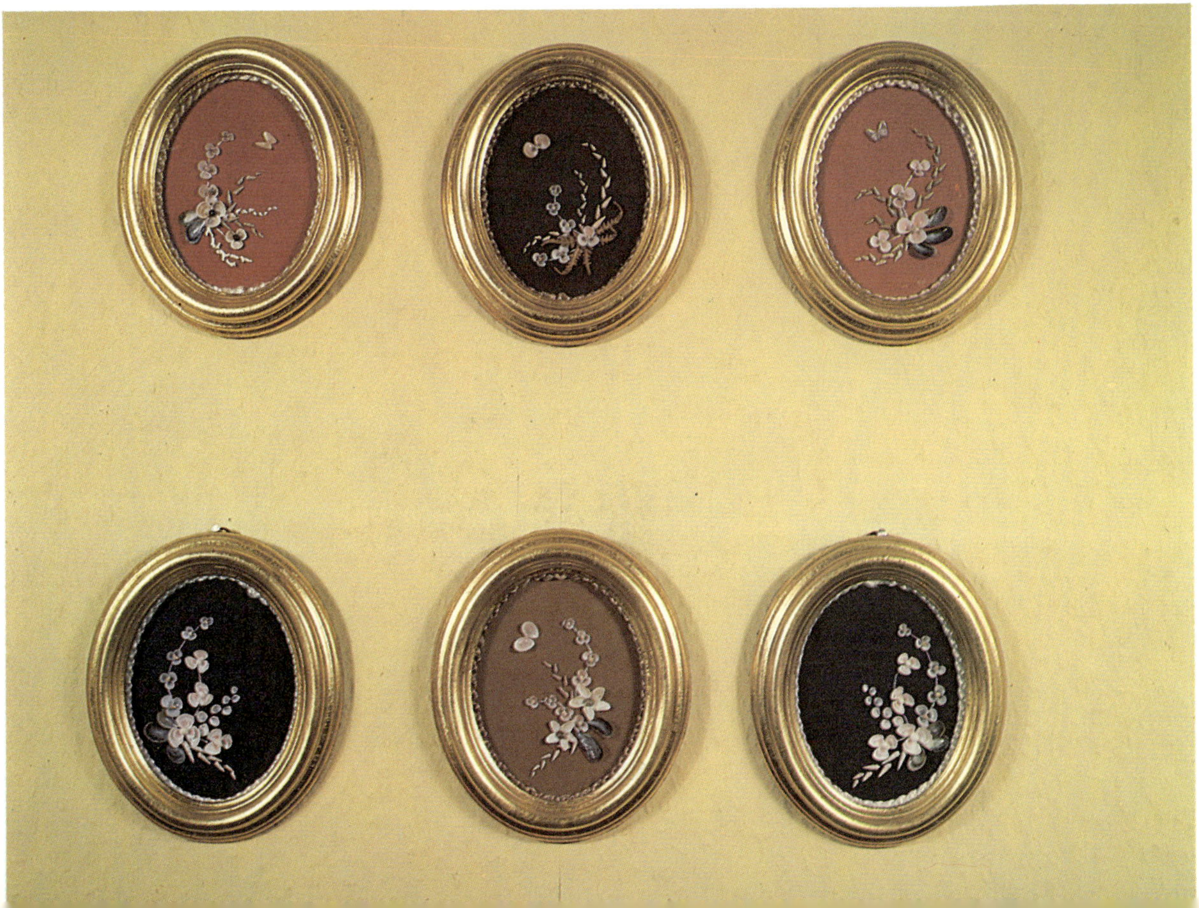

Shell patterns

Making shells into patterns is probably one of the most popular shell design pastimes. This is because they can be made by all age groups being either simple or complex, round, square, or geometrical. All can be very striking. When making a geometrical design always find the centre first, by measuring, and then work outwards, but remember to ensure that you have an adequate amount of shells, because you may not be able to change the shell types half-way.

Patterns have been demonstrated in this book by two designs.

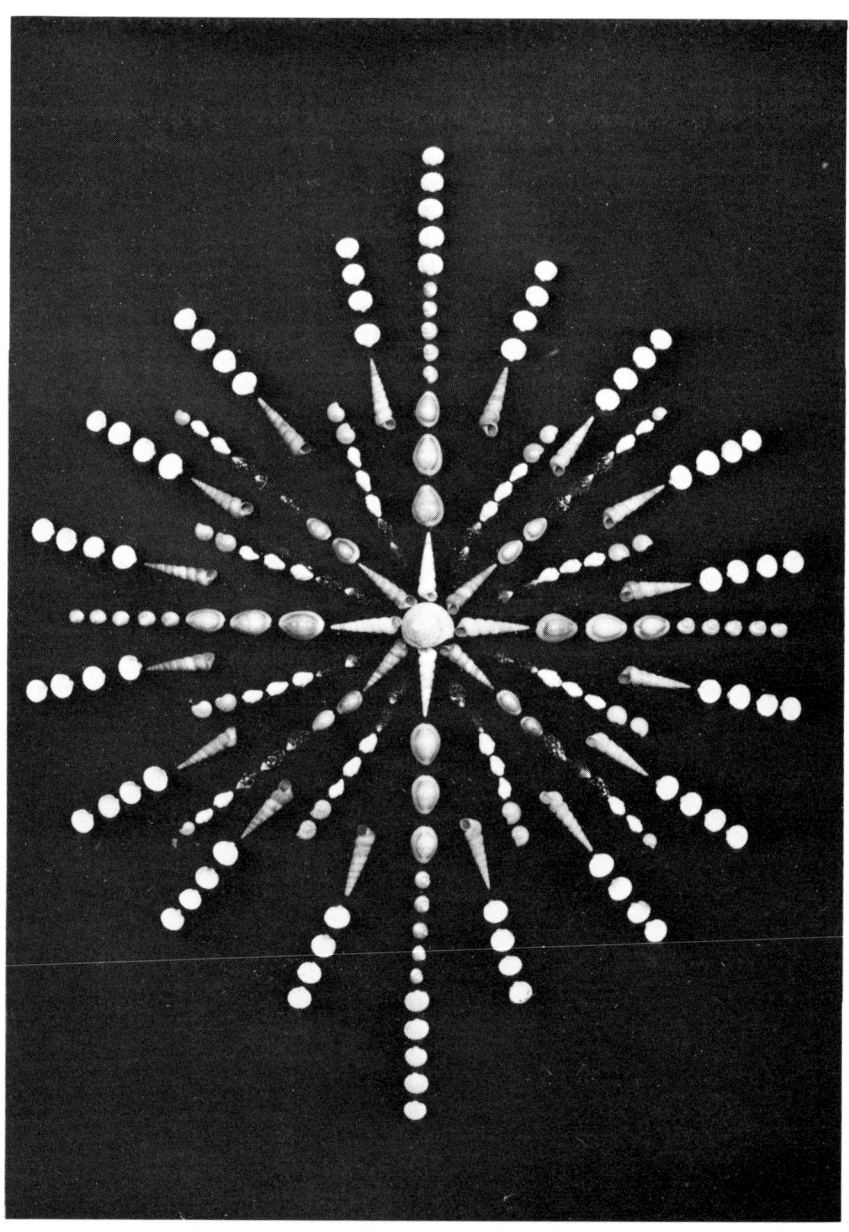

A circular pattern.

Circular pattern 45cm × 62cm (18in × 25in)

The pattern in the photograph on page 62 is designed to be striking and eye catching. In the very centre of the pattern is a pinkish Top Shell; radiating outwards from this are pink and white Auger Shells, followed by black Planaxis which give a feeling of depth to the picture, as if the surrounding spines are coming from deep behind the centre-piece.

Gold Ringer Cowries act as four solid lines, whilst white Dove Shells and Umbonium lead to the outer ring of Auger Shells. Finally the white Cockle shells and Pearly Trochuses make splendid spreading tendrils, resulting in the starkness required.

The design was set upon a finely woven brown linen material and mounted in a gold metal frame.

Tendril pattern 63cm × 16cm (25in × 6.5in)

This picture was made to hang on a low wall and so it had to be long and narrow see plate 3. The background material is a rough, blue hessian, giving the picture the texture needed to throw out the shape of the smooth shells.

In the centre I have placed a bleached fish bone with a crab shell top mounted upon it — spreading out from here are broken gastropods, Tusk Shells, white Cockle shells, Auger Shells, Bubble Shells and a number of dark brown pebbles.

The broken gastropods and grey Top Shells spread out from the centre in long tendrils, again adding width to the picture. From this pattern you can see how easily other materials can be used in conjunction with shells. An unusual wooden frame has been used for this picture. The wood has been painted with a brown, mottled paint so as to pick out the darker coloured shells.

Contrast and toning

So far in this chapter we have looked at examples of shell designs which have contained various colours in the same picture. Alternatively you can use just one colour on either a contrasting or toning background. For example, all tones of pink shells on a brown background. Using these techniques can result in an attractive and striking design.

Before the picture is begun, make sure you have ample shells in the colour you desire and if possible quite a variety of types, otherwise your design could become boring.

Red and white contrasting collage 40cm × 54cm (16in × 21.5in)

Contrasting designs can be one of the most effective techniques in the use of shells. The red and white design in plate 4 is a good example of this technique. Of course the shells and background must really contrast with each other, not clash with one another; there is a subtle difference, and when the clash occurs it is immediately apparent.

Although white shells on red was the main theme here, a number of off-white Dog Whelks were added so as to relieve the starkness a little. Bubble Shells were also carefully chosen for their beige spots, adding a little subtle colour and interest to the picture.

All the petalled flowers were kept to the white theme. White Scallops together with white Saddle Oysters make a beautiful centre-piece. From this flow stems of white Common Cockle Shells and the beautiful Bubble Shell flowers lead on to the Baltic Tellin roses.

This picture also illustrates two of the many uses that the sea washed, broken gastropods can serve. They make lovely curling flower centres and can also be used as foliage.

The design was mounted on dark gold hessian and then placed in a gold leaf wooden frame.

Blue toning collage

Plate 5 is an example of using background material and shells which tone and blend with each other. The material in this particular case is a linen of medium rough texture.

The blue Mussel Shells lend themselves perfectly both in shape and colour to the centre-piece, and by using only cream and black as the other colours in the design, the blue theme was kept. Other shells used in this picture were cream Dog Whelks, blue tinged Banded Wedge Shells, beige Common Limpets and black Planaxis.

A small number of Rose Petal Shells were used to give depth and a little interest to the picture, otherwise it could have easily become dull and uninventive.

I decided to frame this picture in a frame that would continue the blue theme and so I chose stainless steel.

Pink and brown 40cm × 60cm (16in × 24in)

This particular collage was made by using a pink and brown theme. The design is mounted on a brown suedette material which has been sewn onto hardboard. See plate 6.

The focal point has been deliberately set low in the design and has been made of Augers and Pelicans Foot Shells. Radiating outwards from the centre are stems of pink Baltic Tellin roses, together with wavy tendrils of Dog Whelks, Rough Winkles and Umbonium Shells.

A bronze metal was used to frame this picture, which supplements the browns in the picture and tones in very effectively.

Overcrowding

As I have mentioned earlier in the book, it is very easy to overcrowd

a picture and use wrongly shaped and coloured shells. The photograph on page 64 is a perfect example of these mistakes.

Blue Mussel shells have been used for the centre flowers, but as you can see they are far too large and some are even broken and chipped. The shells have also been worked too closely to the edge of the background and so when the design is framed the result looks vastly overcrowded and squashed.

Limpet and Atlantic Slipper shells would have been fine as trailing flowers had smaller, more colourful specimens been used, but again they are far too large and drab.

A Baltic Tellin Shell used as a butterfly, is normally an ideal way to balance a picture, but here it appears to be totally out of place because again the shell was too large and clumsy.

The black background material would have been better if it had been used to contrast with the shells. Instead the whole colour scheme is too bland and unimaginative.

Chapter 5

A PERSONAL PORTFOLIO

It has only been possible to touch upon a few of the various ways in which shells can be used. There are numerous other ways which have not been mentioned, but I am sure that once you have had more experience, you will find your own inspiration.

I have spent many happy hours collecting and creating with sea shells, both as a hobby and as a full time occupation, and I hope that you too will find enjoyment in this craft.

This chapter contains a collection of works which were commissions, so they were designed using colours and textures which were suited to the existing decor of the room where the picture was to be placed.

It is impossible to give full details of how these designs were made, because of the vast amount of different materials used. Therefore, each work will be accompanied by brief details of colour, texture and the names of shells used.

We shall start by looking at three shell designs, all of which have been used in picture form. The shells were largely intended to represent flowers, but they have not been arranged as you would expect to find them in real flower arrangements. I have tried to give the effect of the flowers growing out from their background and, by using them in conjunction with other shells which have been used in an imaginative fashion, the final result is almost abstract.

When making designs of this size, I always start with a centre-piece, which is usually something quite solid, giving me a base on which to build the rest of the design. It is essential for the position and colour, of the centre-piece to be correct, because the viewers attention is always caught by this part of the composition.

Front cover collage 33cm × 59cm (13in × 23.5in)

In the composition on the front cover of this book and in the photograph on page 68 you will see how the use of flower sprays can create movement within the design. It is always easier to do this with small, delicate shells because large shells have a thicker, more solid appearance. Larger shells are, however, ideal for single flowers which do not grow in sprays.

A solid centre-piece has been created by using cream and bronze Saddle Oysters, from out of which the smaller flowers flow in sprays. For example, the roses made from pink Baltic Tellins Shells and Cockle Shell flowers which resemble crab apple blossom.

Small Banded Wedge Shells make perfect daisies because of their size and colouring. These were small and pale which meant that a considerable number could be grouped together, providing the balance necessary for that particular part of the design. Banded Striped Dog Whelks and black Rough Winkle Shells, looking as though they are growing from the centre, wind their way up to the top of the background, adding height to the design.

The design has been placed upon a light brown, cotton suedette material which can be brushed to give the same effect as suede. A gold metal frame, with a black inset completes the design.

Horizontal design 65cm × 34cm (26in × 13.5in)

This design involves the full use of movement but it is also symmetrical. See photograph on page 69.

The outer petals of the centre flower have been made from three beige Saddle Oysters; the inner petals are made from bronze and black Saddle Oysters. Two similar but smaller flowers on each side complete the central composition. This is the point at which this picture was started and from this trail stems of pink Baltic Tellin roses and some small flowers made from Cockle shells.

Gastropods form the rest of the picture and act as spikes of strange, imaginary flowers. Again a metal frame was used to complete the design.

Vertical design

This composition was designed for a particular situation and colour scheme. Bronze Saddle Oysters form the centre flowers with tendrils of white and beige flowers spreading outwards.

The picture is given length by using sprays of white Dog Whelks and Baltic Tellins roses. Small white Cowrie shells emerge from the centre resembling wheat grains. Broken, sea washed gastropods give a pretty leaf-like effect. See plate 7.

The pale shades of the shells are contrasted by the darker colour of the blue-black mussel shells. Some of the other shells used are Atlantic Slipper Shells, Prickly Cockles and Pearly Trochuses.

I chose a black background to contrast and give the whole design a striking effect. It is completed with a gold metal frame.

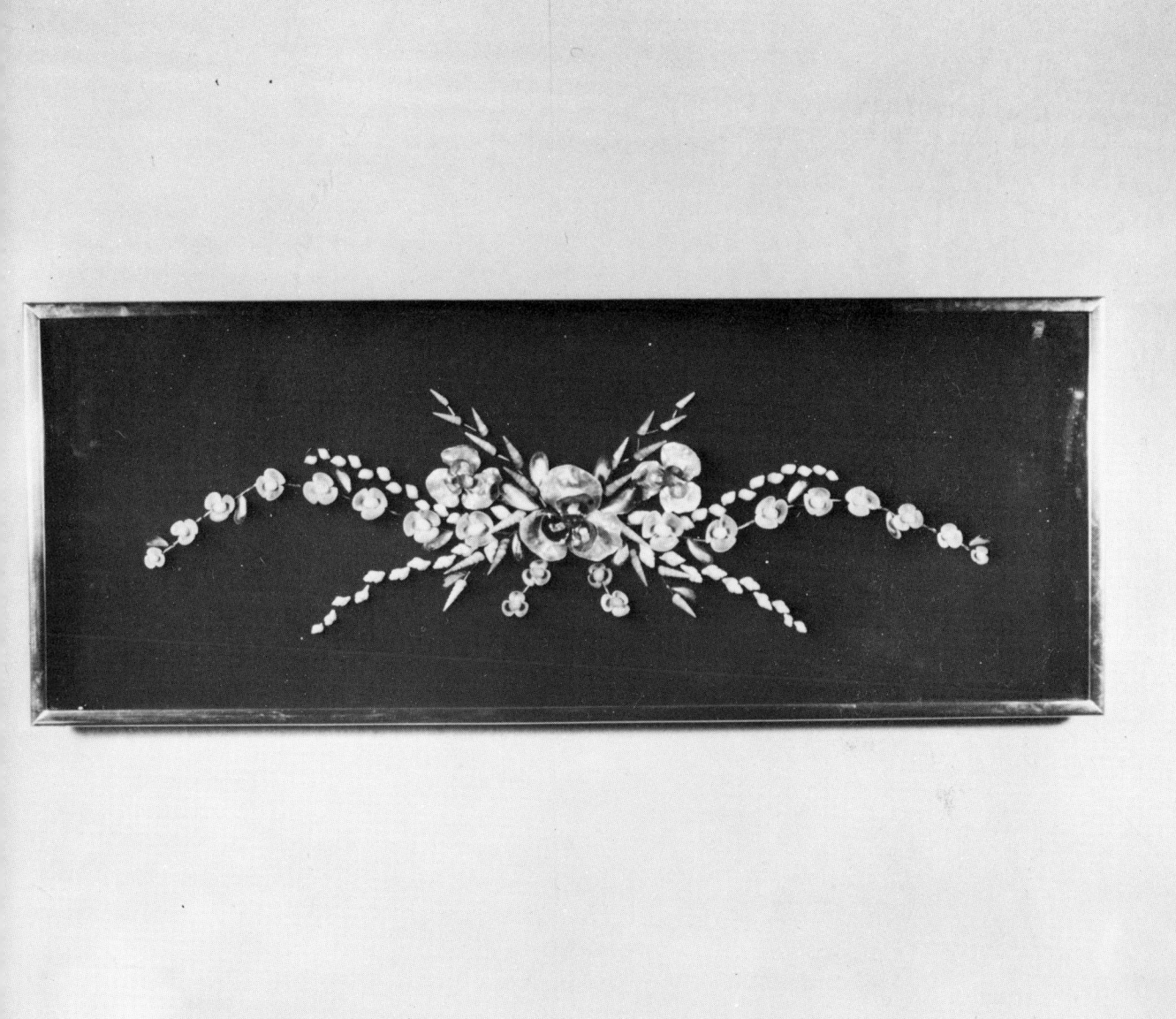

Opposite: Front cover collage

Above: Horizontal design

69

Other types of presentation

Shell pictures and designs do not always have to be put into a picture frame and hung on the wall. They can be utilised in various ways and put into different settings. The next three pieces exemplify this — a room divider, coffee table and fire screen.

Room divider 158cm × 63cm (63in × 25in)

This composition is extremely varied, both in the shells used and the types of flowers made with them. It is set upon a background of dark brown cotton on hardboard. See plate 9.

The theme wild flowers in a hedgerow. Because of the size of the design, it would have been impossible to carry the shells along the bottom in a continuous line, as this would have appeared far too solid. The design was therefore broken up by making an arrangement in each bottom corner and working towards the centre. These were both started in the same way as any other picture, with the centre-piece, and then both designs were developed from that point.

In order to try and simulate wild flowers I used every colour, size and shape of shell I had available. Roses made from pink and yellow Baltic Tellin Shells; daisies from Banded Wedge Shells; irises made from Scallop Shells; hanging racemes of yellow bloom made from yellow Flat Winkle Shells and many, many more. In all twenty-five different types of shells were used in this picture, including Rough and Common Cockle shells, black and variegated Nerites, Nut Shells, Ear Shells, Spotted Cowries, blue Rayed Limpets, Trough Shells, Razor Shells, Saddle Oysters and blue Mussel Shells.

Other materials, such as pebbles, coral and seaweed have been used to help produce a base from which the shell flowers may 'grow' naturally. Small groups of coloured Thin Tellin butterflies complete the scene.

Coffee table Plate 8 47cm × 91cm × 47cm (19in × 36.5in × 19in)

Setting a design into a table was a completely new idea and far different from anything I had previously done, thus several problems occurred. For example, it meant that the design would be seen from a completely different angle. It would not be seen from the usual, eye level position, but would be low and so looked down upon. Because it was a table it would be viewed from all sides and so there could be no top or bottom to the shell design. I therefore split the design, using two smaller compositions in opposite corners. In one corner, a design was made from Bronze Saddle Oysters, Limpets and dark Cockle shells. The composition in the opposite corner is slightly larger and lighter in colour than its counterpart. Light bronze Saddle Oysters form the centre-piece and spiky Tusk Shells emerge like thorns from the stems. White Cockle Shells, Atlantic Slipper Shells and spotted Cowries complete the rest of the design which spreads up and across the background in beautiful trails.

The complete design has been set upon a dark green material, on hardboard. This was then set into a beech wood table.

Fire screen Plate 10 43cm × 48cm (17in × 19in)

For this particular design shells of very bright colours were used. As usual with a picture I started at the centre, with bronze and black Saddle Oysters. Dark Cockle Shell flowers were used to add strength to the centre and flowing from these are trails of Prickly Cockle Shells and yellow and orange Baltic Tellins.

Fire screen

A large group of mauve Banded Wedge Shell daisies add colour harmony and balance to the left of the picture. Dark mauve Donax Shells and pink Baltic Tellin Shells add depth of colour to the picture. All the flowers in the design have been 'arranged' on long stems to produce a trailing effect.

Banded Wedge Shell butterflies complete the picture which has been set on a natural hessian background and then mounted into a black, wrought iron frame.

Abstract designs

Abstract paintings either motivate or leave one cold. Some are far too complex to understand unless one happens to be an art critic. On the other hand, abstract collages, whether made from fabrics or as in this case natural materials, are usually very interesting. They are also very rewarding to design. Abstract collages are somewhat more difficult to make because the shapes are already formed for the artist by nature.

More than any other type of design, abstracts require texture, colour and shape to balance and create harmony throughout the design.

Abstract seascape Plate 11 61cm × 61cm (24.5in × 24.5in)

A vast range of materials has been used in this design, far too numerous to list. All of the materials are within a colour spectrum of white through to brown and the background is of natural hessian so keeping the colour scheme. Most of these materials have been collected over a number of years from various sea shores until eventually there was a large enough assortment to make a picture. Dried leaves, ferns, fishbones, stones, coral and broken gastropods are just a few of the components.

Miniatures

Both Hilliard and Oliver, the great Elizabethan Miniaturists, were fast in realizing the fascination of miniature objects, a fascination which seems to impel people to look at and collect them.

Shells are no exception to this rule. They are absolutely enchanting when in the miniature form. The designs are made in the same manner as the larger ones, but all the work has to be done with the aid of a pair of tweezers and a lot of patience.

It is even more important that the colours and shapes balance and harmonise with each other in these small designs, but it is considerably more difficult to achieve movement and flowing patterns on this scale due to the size of shells and the lack of background available.

Miniature ovals Plate 12 12cm × 15cm (5in × 6in)

The ovals on the reverse cover of this book and on pages 73-77 are made with shells that are no bigger than 1.5cm (0.6in) in length. In fact most are a great deal smaller.

Almost all the shells that have been used previously in this book can be obtained in miniature. They can be found and collected on any coast line, but sharp observation and eyesight is essential. Among some of my favourites are Nut Shells, Tellins, all types of Winkles and Rose Petals, which are a member of the Tellin family. All background materials are exactly the same as used in the larger designs.

A selection of Miniature ovals, showing examples of some of the most useful small shells.

Pill boxes

These small boxes have been absolutely encrusted with tiny sea shells and again all of the work has to be carried out with tweezers.

Most of the shells used here are slightly larger than those used in the miniature pictures. When working on something as small and complex as these boxes, it is important to decide upon the pattern and shells you wish to use before you begin, because you cannot just place the shells at random, or you will quickly find you have a disaster on your hands. Pearly Trochuses, Nut Shells, Dove Shells, Limpet and Tusk Shells, flat Winkles and Rose Petals combine to make up the bulk of shells used.

Pill boxes

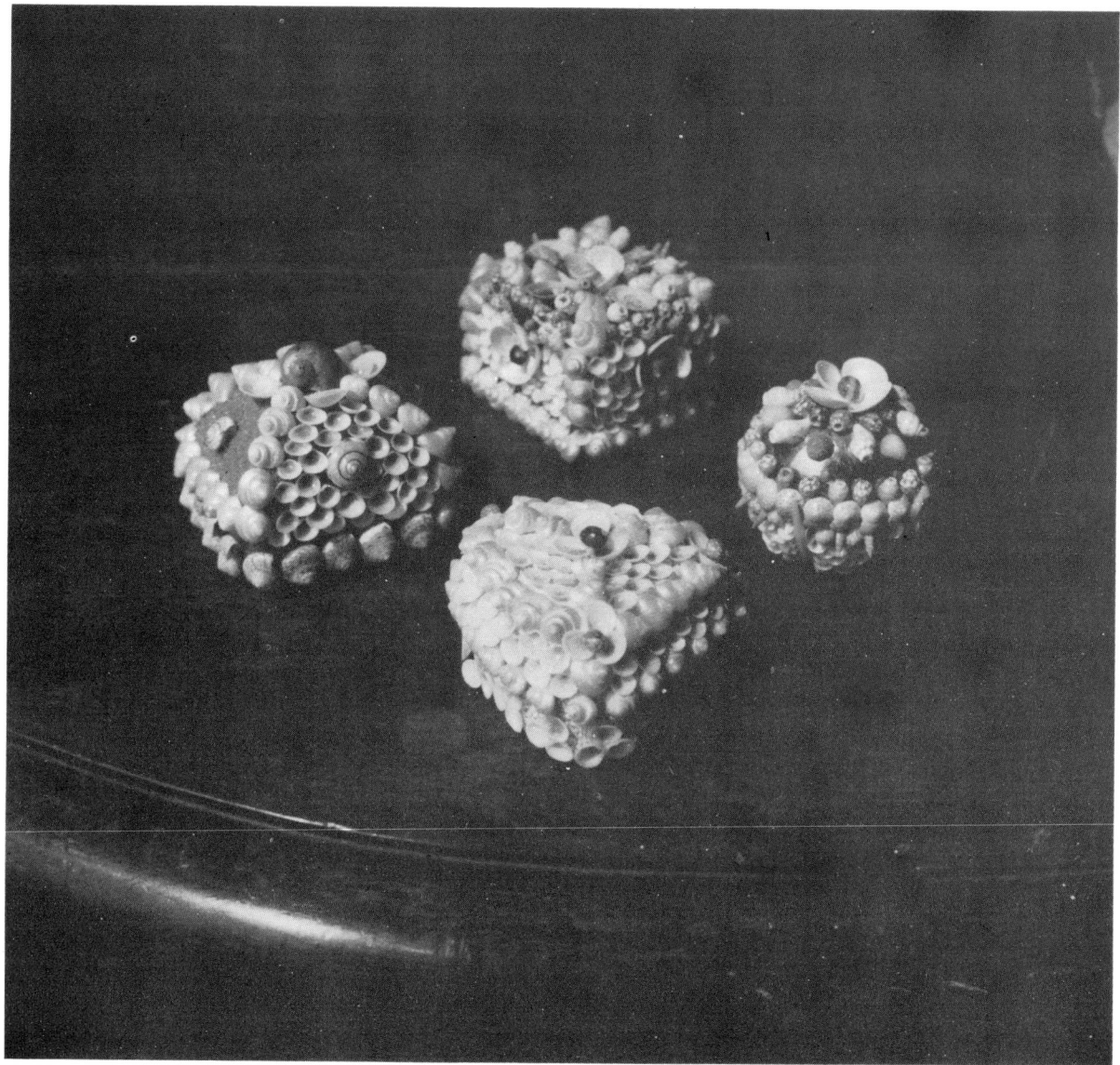

Some interesting facts

Anthropologists believe that the fossilised remains of certain mollusc species found with primitive human remains, indicate trade routes of considerable distances. The earliest known collection of trade shells dates approximately 25,000 years ago and these were found in some French caves. They were tropical shells which could not have survived in European waters. Exotic species such as the Red Helmet Snail suggests European trading with Indian and Pacific Ocean countries.

The Australian Trumpet Shell is the largest gastropod in the world, with recorded measurements reaching up to 60cm (2ft) long.

The Giant Clam is the largest bivalve in the world and it can reach lengths of 1.50m (4.5ft). It is found on the Indo-Pacific coral reefs. Their shells are so thick and heavy that it takes two men to carry each valve. The heaviest recorded pair weighed 263kg (579 pounds).

A yellow liquid, which is obtained from the Dye Murex, when treated turns to a purple dye. Evidence has been found on the island of Crete to suggest it was used as a dye as early as 1600 BC. It also had great value. During the reign of the Roman Augustus, a pound of dyed wool sold for 1,000 denari — a sum now approximately equal to £350.

The Noble Pen Shell attaches itself to other objects by feathery threads called byssals. These threads are strong, fine and of a bronze gold colour and the Sicilians used to spin them into beautiful, golden silk, which, up until the late nineteenth century, was used in the manufacture of gloves, stockings and caps.

The beautiful Thorny Oysters are the most ostentatious of all the bivalves, with long thin spines reaching a length of up to 15cm (6in), but they are not in actual fact oysters at all. They are members of the Scallop family.

Thin shelled Cymbium Volutes are unique in harbouring their young in their oviduct until they are ready to emerge and crawl out as fully developed, miniature volutes.

Shipworms are world wide and they devote their entire life to boring holes in wood. Many ships in the past have succumbed to the ravages of this member of the Clam family. It can penetrate a 15cm (6in) thick plank in less than a year.

INDEX